T H E

Future of
Warfare

NEW YORK · LONDON

THE
Future of
Warfare

BEVIN ALEXANDER

 W · W · NORTON & COMPANY

ISBN 0-393-03780-8

W. W. Norton & Company, Inc., 500 Fifth Avenue, New York, N.Y. 10110
W. W. Norton & Company Ltd., 10 Coptic Street, London WC1A 1PU

Contents

Contents

Introduction

WHEN I COMMENCED WRITING this book, I was well aware of the famous line from the English economist, Lord Keynes: "The inevitable never happens. It is the unexpected always." No one, of course, can predict the future of warfare with certainty. Yet great events in the late twentieth century have given us reason to believe that we can prophesy with some accuracy what sorts of conflicts are likely to occur, how wars are likely to be fought, and which ones will involve the United States—at least for a generation ahead.

This book examines the degree to which changes in war brought on worldwide by theory and practice during this century will affect war in the next century. It also studies the influence technology has had and may have on military strategy, battle tactics, and unit structure. But, since the greatest challenges will be borne by the United States, the last superpower, this book focuses primarily on what it will encounter and the sorts of wars it will have to fight in the decades ahead.

With the disintegration of the Soviet Union in the early 1990s, the discipline that had held the world firmly in two antagonistic ideological camps abruptly snapped. For a euphoric moment much of the world believed that the principal divisions on the planet had been healed and that we could look forward to a peaceful, cooperative future.

We quickly learned how wrong we were. Ethnic, religious, and nationalistic conflicts that had been suppressed for generations by East-West bipolarity suddenly reemerged throughout the world, especially in the former Soviet Union and among its erstwhile satellites. Witches' caldrons that had been stewing disagreements, rivalries, and hates, sometimes for centuries, abruptly boiled over. The list of social upheavals seems endless. Among others are clan, tribal, and ethnic battles in Africa; religious disputes in Africa, Asia and Europe; racial collisions in South Africa; deep divisions between rich and poor in Latin America, and ethnic conflict in the former Yugoslavia, Turkey, Iraq, Azerbaidzhan, Georgia, Spain, and elsewhere.

The United States will avoid most of these largely internecine conflicts. It also will avoid wars over political ideology. The repudiation of Communism by nearly all peoples, including its tacit rejection by the Chinese, has left no ideology strong enough to challenge capitalism and market economies.

Russia constitutes no greater danger than any other great power. The emergence of jingoistic elements there have aroused fears of aggression. Russia may project itself more strongly onto the world stage, but few Russians have ambitions to expand out of northern Eurasia.

It is inconceivable that any nation controlled by sensible rulers will resort to nuclear warfare. Use of a nuclear device likely would bring instant retaliation which could accelerate beyond human capacity to control, making much of the earth uninhabitable.

An irrational dictator might use the bomb, and there's

the chance that a terrorist organization might secure a device and plant it somewhere, perhaps in a large city. This would bring on a catastrophe, but rational rulers would not automatically resort to nuclear holocaust. Instead, likely using precision strikes, nuclear or otherwise, they would attempt to destroy the dictator, his weapons and his scientists, or they could try to destroy the places in other countries where the guilty terrorists find refuge. Retribution is so certain that only a completely unstable, nihilistic ruler would risk his own and his country's destruction. As a consequence, nations are likely to face only conventional, nonnuclear wars.

Nevertheless, the United States will encounter the continued threat of war. The principal cause will be the revival of aspirations for power by avaricious nations or ambitious leaders. Lust for power has been the bane of mankind at least from Neolithic times. Desire for power is closely tied to economic issues. Disputes over possession of the earth's riches and resources have always been the primary reasons for wars. For nearly fifty years the East and West held economic conflicts in check by dividing the world's resources between them. With the end of the Cold War this expedient lost its validity.

BEVIN ALEXANDER

THE
Future of
Warfare

ONE

American Strategy for the New Era

T HE UNITED STATES is in a new world that, despite appearances, is much like the old. Its only truly dangerous enemy for nearly half a century, the Soviet Union, has ceased to exist both as an empire and as a threat. The remaining dangers to peace are painful and depressing, but minor. Nevertheless, American strategic concerns have remained the same. The United States has the identical obligation that has molded its history from the beginning: security of American territory, people, economy, and way of life.

The United States, as the only surviving superpower, has the strength to guard its security, as well as to influence profoundly the kind of world all people will inhabit in the future. This world will determine what sorts of wars the United States will fight, and how it will fight them.

Although the planet today seems awash with internal and external conflict, only two principal types of international dangers are likely to threaten American security: (1) attempts by one or more powers to seize vital industrial commodities like oil, and (2) attempts by some power to gain hegemony or dominance in Eurasia, or in part of it.

Neither danger is imminent, but either could occur. Either would probably require the projection of American power onto another continent. The United States may get involved in other types of conflict, but these two are what the nation's military must be prepared to confront.

The fear that a power would gain hegemony in an important part of Eurasia has guided politics and generated wars for more than three centuries. It forced Britain, Austria, Russia, and Prussia to battle Napoleon Bonaparte; required Britain, France, Russia, and the United States to challenge Germany in two world wars; led to a war with Japan; spawned the anti-Soviet alliance system in the Cold War, and produced wars against three supposed surrogates of the Soviet Union: North Korea, China, and North Vietnam.[1]

It is a permanent danger because a regional or continental

1. (In notes throughout the book, some references give only the last name of the author or editor. Works referred to are cited in full in the Selected Bibliography. References not listed in the bibliography are cited in full where they appear in the notes. Numbers in notes refer to pages.) Both the Korean War and the Vietnam War illustrate that fear of a power gaining hegemony over a region is as important in generating wars as the reality. The United States feared that North Korea and China were acting on orders from the Soviet Union to gain positions in northeast Asia for an attack against Japan. Likewise the United States believed that the Soviets and Chinese were attempting through local Communists to take over, first, Vietnam, then other states in Southeast Asia (the "falling-domino theory"). We later realized both fears were unfounded and that the Korean and Vietnam conflicts were primarily national wars to unify the two countries by force. China's participation in both wars was to prevent American forces coming against its frontier. China feared that the United States entertained ideas of reinstating its ally, Nationalist China, in mainland China. The Chinese Communists pushed the Nationalists onto Taiwan in 1949.

hegemonic power can create a global navy and threaten the United States directly.

From the late 1600s to World War I, Britain sought, by means of a "balance of power" in Europe, to prevent the rise of a continental navy that could contest the seas with the Royal Navy. Britain tried, in most cases with success, to aid weaker powers in their conflicts with the stronger, and thereby keep the European states so embroiled in indecisive disputes with each other that none had sufficient resources to create a navy capable of defeating the British fleet. Napoleon's challenge came closest to success, but Horatio Nelson destroyed his fleet at Trafalgar in 1805 and guaranteed that the French empire would not extend overseas. When Napoleon failed in his invasion of Russia in 1812, the collapse of his empire began.

After World War I, the United States began to take on the naval role that a declining Britain was laying down. By the end of World War II, the U.S. Navy greatly outclassed other fleets. Today, it has more than half of the earth's naval tonnage, and its ships are far superior to the warships of other nations.[2]

The United States must keep another power from building a great navy, because control of the seas is imperative to American security. The navy is the principal means the United States has to prevent the incursion of a power from the Eastern Hemisphere into the Western Hemisphere. A

2. The U.S. Navy's combat power is greater than all the rest of the world's naval power put together. The main ingredient of naval power is the aircraft carrier. The United States has fourteen, each carrying 80 to 100 aircraft. The nearest competitor is France with two, each carrying forty aircraft.

fundamental element of American strategy is to maintain our hegemony in North and South America. That is the purpose behind the Monroe Doctrine of 1823.[3] That is why the United States can tolerate no power capable of challenging it in the Americas, and why it must prevent the rise of a hegemonic power in Eurasia.

The United States finally, but reluctantly, accepted this strategy in World Wars I and II, but only after Germany had inflicted deep wounds on its enemies and come close to dominating the continent.

The question may be asked: why do we need to worry about Eurasia now? Isn't the Soviet Union dead, and aren't all other major powers either allies, like Germany, Britain,

3. Control of the Western Hemisphere is the cornerstone of American national security. It is based, not on our right, but on our survival. We decided early in our national history that the presence of great powers in the Western Hemisphere constituted a grave threat to the existence of the United States. We relied on the British navy to keep out European powers until our navy became the greatest in the world. We see the Western Hemisphere as an island, and our country, like Britain, as an insular, not a continental, power. Hence, we cannot allow any other world power to share this island with us and must prevent any Eurasian global navy from lodging here. This explains the American resolve to maintain the greatest navy, our occasional retreats into isolationism "behind our oceans," and our uncompromising reaction to any incursion into the hemisphere. Only the American Civil War prevented us from challenging France's occupation of Mexico in the 1860s and U.S. opposition led to the French evacuation in 1867. The Zimmermann telegram of 1917, a heavy-handed German effort to enlist Mexico in a war with the United States on the promise that Germany would restore lands taken away in the Mexican War, was one of the principal reasons we fought Germany in World War I. If Premier Nikita Khrushchev had not removed missiles from Cuba, we would have gone to war against the Soviet Union in 1962. For a concise analysis of the Monroe Doctrine, see Julius W. Pratt, *A History of United States Foreign Policy* (New York: Prentice-Hall, 1955), 166, 169–84, 243–44, 289, 339–52, 415, 423, 608, 614–16. See also Barbara W. Tuchman, *The Zimmermann Telegram* (New York: Macmillan, 1958; New York: Ballantine, 1979, 1985).

and Japan, or uninterested in territorial expansion, like China and France?

The answer, of course, is that today none of these powers poses a danger. But no one can predict the future. Also, as we saw in the case of Iraq, smaller powers can seize important resources, or, as in the case of Iran, can threaten to destabilize a region by arming themselves heavily.

Aggression grows in unsettled or disorderly times and explodes in a power vacuum. We already are seeing evidence of disorder. Hopefully the cases will be resolved and no harm will come from them. But they are examples of the sorts of problems that can lead to great upheavals: a neo-Nazi revival in Germany, right-wing movements in France, the emergence of xenophobic tendencies in Russia, and proposals to limit Japan's heavy inroads into foreign markets.

Hard economic times engender aggression, internal or external or both. Hunger and despair of the people begat the French Revolution of 1789. That upheaval transformed Western society and made possible Napoleon Bonaparte's attempt to conquer the world. Adolf Hitler rode to power on the resentment of the German people to the economic burdens imposed on them by the victors of World War I and on their sufferings in the great Depression of the 1930s. Japan's quest for empire accelerated when its export markets evaporated as a result of this same Depression.

All of these aggressions were vastly intensified by the power vacuums in which they occurred. The sclerotic, aristocratic regimes of Europe did not work in concert to contain the ferment of the French Revolution and were overwhelmed. Hitler faced a hesitant, indecisive Britain and France and an absent United States, and had conquered or dominated all of central Europe before the two Western powers at last reacted. The United States waited until Germany declared war after Japan attacked Pearl Harbor in December 1941. Japan met almost no effective opposition from major powers from 1931 until the summer of 1941, when U.S. President Franklin D. Roosevelt finally cut off trade with the empire. During that period Japan seized Manchuria, much of China proper, and French Indochina, and was moving on Malaya and the East Indies.

History shows that nations, like individuals, react selfishly and often violently to straitened economic or social conditions. In hard times they seldom work in concert to achieve a general solution for everyone, but strive feverishly for national, or personal, salvation. We still cannot predict with certainty when great recessions will occur and how far incomes will fall, and therefore cannot devise remedies before disaster strikes.

To date, the United States has been lucky. In previous incarnations of powers bent on hegemony in Eurasia, other states have borne the brunt of the aggression until the United States summoned up the resolve and the military power to meet the challenge. In World War I, Britain, France, and Russia had been bled white before the United States entered the war. In World War II we waited until we were actually attacked before taking up the cause.

We responded more quickly to the challenge of the Soviet Union, forming an alliance soon after we concluded in 1945 that Joseph Stalin entertained visions of expansion. Swift American action closed off any chance of Soviet aggression without general war.

Today, we must be prepared to respond as quickly. We

won't have the chance to rearm at leisure, as we did in the past.

The United States has no other real choice. It cannot rely on its anti-Soviet alliance to enforce a balance in Eurasia. This American-dominated system has lost its reason for being and will dissolve. Fear of the Soviet Union kept it together. That fear has vanished, and member nations will revert to policies that seek their own, not common, interests.[4]

The United States cannot retreat into some "America First" isolationism behind its oceans, as it did after World War I. This policy came close to conceding the Western world to Adolf Hitler. Without projection of U.S. power into Eurasia, another Hitler could arise. Also, the United States cannot allow other powers to gain control of important industrial commodities or the world's oil supply. It especially must protect the principal petroleum reserves, located in the Persian Gulf region.[5]

4. When former satellite eastern European states tried to get into the North Atlantic Treaty Organization (NATO) in 1993–94, the United States resisted on the sensible ground that the only possible enemy of NATO was Russia. The Russian president, Boris Yeltsin, complained that neither NATO nor the ex-satellites should be targeting his country, since it no longer represented a threat. Indeed, to insist that Russia is a threat would fuel historic Russian fears of encirclement by outside powers.

5. Therefore, the "America First—and Second, and Third" proposal by commentator and 1992 presidential candidate Patrick Buchanan cannot be American strategy. Buchanan expressed his theory in *National Interest* 19 (Spring 1990): 77–82. America First theories hold that the United States should ignore international security problems unless they threaten the United States directly, and prod other states to fill security roles abandoned by the United States. The United States can't rely on such states to follow American interests. See also Lt. Gen. William E. Odom, *America's Military Revolution* (Washington, D.C.: American University Press, 1993), 22–27.

These strategic imperatives obligate the United States not only to maintain its navy as the greatest in the world, but to provide its air force and army with highest-level technology and weapons to be capable of intervening effectively wherever any power threatens the political or economic balance. The very definition of a superpower is that it possesses the ability to project decisive force in intercontinental interventions.[6] In most cases the United States will operate as did the British: forming alliances with threatened states to prevent a single power from achieving dominance.

President George Bush implemented this strategy when he organized a coalition of nations to restore Kuwait to its rulers after Iraq invaded it in 1990. Bush called it the "new world order." It was not, but rather a new application of an old strategy. If the Iraqi dictator, Saddam Hussein, had succeeded, he would have controlled much of the world's oil. Although this would not have upset the power balance in Eurasia, it would have greatly affected the price and availability of oil, and would have disrupted world economies. Also statesmen remembered that Hitler commenced his aggressions slowly, but proceeded from one success to another, until he nearly controlled Europe. They resolved to stop Saddam before he got too far.

During the Cold War, Americans saw their strategy as protecting all nations against domination by a world power. To some degree, the United States still perceives itself as continuing to guard the free world. But today the line between free and unfree has been blurred, and the line between rich and poor has more validity. Other nations may now dispute an American role as protector. The United States

6. Friedman and Lebard, 191.

may keep new Soviet Unions from arising, and stop Saddam Husseins from seizing the world's oil, but who will keep the United States from exploiting or perhaps conquering them? With no Soviet Union threatening, other powers may regard U.S. control of the seas as a device to advance American interests. They certainly viewed Britain in this light when it ruled the waves, and with justification, because Britain used its invincible navy and its less-powerful army to advance its own economic and political interests.

The United States may exploit its superpower position, but it cannot conquer the world. Like Britain of yore, it lacks one essential element: manpower, and, most significantly, the willingness to expend it in conquest. It cannot master Eurasia by force, because American manpower is far too small to mount the kinds of military operations necessary to subdue it or even to establish springboards there. Two wars on the supercontinent in the past forty-five years, in Korea and Vietnam, have demonstrated this fact. Conflicts with great land powers—because they can't be resolved quickly—tend to become wars of attrition with high casualties. Nations with great manpower reserves can tolerate such losses far better than the United States, which has always abhorred large numbers of killed and wounded. Therefore, the United States must couple its relatively small army with the manpower of allies to keep a balance of power.

Today the balance of power in Eurasia seems assured. Along with the demise of the Soviet Union has come the rise of powerful states or groups of states: the European Union, China, and Japan. These powers, plus Russia, are likely to remain in dynamic tension. If the United States joins with other powers to block any state that adopts an aggressive policy, the power balance is likely to be maintained. This means that big wars, like the world wars whose causes and effects dominated the twentieth century, are extremely unlikely to recur. In their place will be smaller wars, with smaller aims, but not necessarily less vicious.

One of the major unanswered questions is what will happen to world free trade. Many in the American foreign-policy establishment have tried to assure themselves that free trade, which the United States fostered as an integral part of the anti-Soviet alliance system, can become the basis for a permanent international economic system. Open trade would discourage powers or groups of powers from creating their own closed markets and sources of raw materials. Closed regions might give members economic self-sufficiency, or autarky, but they also would create important trade and political zones that would exclude outsiders and divide the world.

The United States is moving away from free trade. Whether it will go very far remains to be seen. During the Cold War, it protected free trade with military power it paid for and it suffered economically as a result—opening its markets to Japan and other countries and finding its industries were less competitive, especially against Japan, because the American economy had to support military costs through taxes while the Japanese economy did not.

The United States no longer is satisfied with this arrangement. It has inaugurated steps against Japan, whose economy expanded enormously under the protection of American military power and which has made deep penetrations into the American market.[7] It also has voted for the North American Free Trade Agreement (NAFTA), which seeks to

7. Bob Davis and Jacob M. Schlesinger, "Trade War? Unlikely, But Shifting Relations Do Increase the Risk," *Wall Street Journal*, February 18, 1994, A1.

limit imports from outsiders, thereby emulating the European Union which has pursued a similar policy. These and other protectionist tendencies imply overt or covert interference with free trade.[8]

The United States does have, in its navy, the kind of power that Britain exercised so effectively for nearly three centuries. Britain couldn't conquer Eurasia, but it could control commerce on the world's oceans and it could project its substantial power wherever its men-of-war could sail, and thus defeat weaker forces. This accounts for Britain's domination of sea trade until World War I, its conquest of India, and its acquisition of underdeveloped lands all around the globe for its empire.

The United States is in position to do the same thing. For example, it can control the Persian Gulf and its oil. Without landing a single soldier on the continent, the United States with its navy can block the Strait of Hormuz and dictate oil prices and supply far more effectively than Saddam Hussein could ever have hoped to do.

With the Soviet Union gone, the United States is certain to seek its own economic interests more forcefully.[9] Some

8. There are strong voices raised against such a U.S.-centered approach. For example, Peter F. Drucker in *The New Realities* (New York: Harper and Row, 1989), 137–38 writes: "If this century has taught one lesson, it is that no part of the developed world prospers unless all do." Given human avarice, however, it's doubtful whether free-traders can overcome protectionism entirely.

9. The United States is likely to support general economic development and trade. But implicit in this concept is that U.S. interests also will be advanced. For example, Gen. Gordon R. Sullivan, army chief of staff, and Lt. Col. James M. Dubik, of his staff, write in *Land Warfare in the 21st Century* (Carlisle Barracks, Pa.: Strategic Studies Institute, U.S. Army War College), February 1993, 6: "U.S. military strategists can expect that their political leaders will seek ways to use the military element of national power—in conjunction with, and usually subordinate to, other elements

elements within the country might try to modify or reduce free trade on the oceans, or require other nations to pay for U.S. protection of the seas by means of controls. One such suggestion is imposition of tolls at strategic points like the Strait of Hormuz or the Strait of Malacca between Sumatra and Malaya. But such a policy would arouse immense anger, and cast the United States as an aggressor with a drive for empire. It would quickly generate an anti-American alliance. A quest for empire would cost the United States far more than it could gain. It's much more likely that the United States will take action against competing nations by means of tariffs or internal controls, especially within NAFTA.[10]

of national power—to promote an environment conducive to political and economic stability abroad. Such uses . . . follow from the fact that American economic security is tied to the world at large. . . ."

10. In November and December 1994, the United States signed three agreements aimed at freer world trade: (1) a plan to bring about a NAFTA-like economic community over the entire Western Hemisphere early in the twenty-first century; (2) a program with seventeen other Pacific Rim nations, including China and Japan, to establish the world's largest free-trade region by 2020; and (3) the new General Agreement on Tariffs and Trade (GATT), signed by 124 nations, which establishes the World Trade Organization, will reduce tariffs by 40 percent and in some cases remove them entirely, and will set up panels to arbitrate trade disputes. Despite these moves, free trade is not guaranteed. Powerful lobbies in most nations seek protection for domestic industries and commerce. Countries often endorse free trade openly, while undermining it covertly. Japan's intricate system of rules and regulations, for example, limits imports far more than tariffs. U.S. steel and textile manufacturers, in the GATT negotiations, protected their markets from unlimited imports, while Japan agreed to permit grain imports only up to 8 percent of domestic consumption. Although international agreements signal a consensus among U.S. and other leaders that free trade is the road to future prosperity, the test will come when economic recessions occur. The lesson of the past has been that nations adopt policies in hard economic times that benefit themselves, even if these policies disrupt world trade. Protectionist practices greatly intensified the worldwide Depression of the 1930s.

Nevertheless, arguments have been made that the United States will restrict sea commerce or access to materials. One argument holds that another war with Japan is coming because the Japanese will be forced to seek control of the sources of their raw materials and markets, just as they attempted to do prior to World War II.[11] When the United States denied them access to these territories, especially in the East Indies and southeast Asia, Japan struck at Pearl Harbor.

Fortunately few experts believe that Japan will be forced to do again what it did in 1941. President Roosevelt assured the Japanese that they could secure all the raw materials they desired on the world market, so long as they renounced aggression. Germany, Britain, France, Italy, and other nations have no guaranteed or captive sources of raw materials today, and no one has argued that they are obligated to go to war to get them.

Closed autarkic empires imply selfish aggression, rather than peaceful trade. The "Greater East Asia Co-Prosperity Sphere" that the Japanese tried to create in 1940 required its members to deliver raw materials to Japan at below market prices and provide Japan with a captive market for its goods. Japan tilted "co-prosperity" decisively in its own favor. The rise of that sort of power in Eurasia is what the United States must oppose, because such a power may be seeking hegemony over Eurasia or over a large portion of it, thereby threatening world peace. No power seeking regional hegemony or autarky will arise because of need, but because of greed.

11. The strongest argument along this line is by Friedman and Lebard in *The Coming War with Japan*.

Although we do not know the precise military opposition we will encounter in the coming years, we can construct
a reasonable set of probabilities. The United States will be
drawn into nearly all clashes anywhere it fears a power is
attempting to achieve hegemony on a regional basis, or, as
in the case of Iraq in 1991, of cornering supplies of a vital
industrial commodity.

The United States will not wait until a power gets as far
as Germany did in World Wars I and II. It will attempt to
stop aggressions while they are relatively small and supposedly containable, as in Korea in 1950 and in Vietnam in the
1960s. In most cases, the United States will seek to work
with allies, as it did against Iraq. Although it will be under
immense pressure to do so, it usually will not intervene in
conflicts between smaller powers unless it fears that one or
more are cat's paws for major powers, or that a power is
seeking to dominate a region.[12]

The United States would resist any attempts by Russia
to reinstitute control over former Soviet satellites in eastern
Europe. Despite the fears of these states, such efforts are
unlikely. To avoid arousing Moscow's historic paranoia that
other states are plotting against Russia, the United States is
moving slowly and hesitantly in bringing the ex-satellites
into the North Atlantic Treaty Organization (NATO).
Anyway, a strong case can be made for a *cordon sanitaire* or
belt of buffer states between the European Union and Russia. Buffers reduce collisions between great powers. The lack

12. Israel is a special case. The large number of Jews in the American
population, plus a great concern for preserving a home for the Jewish
people, means that the United States will continue to support Israel
against efforts of Moslem groups to wipe it out. Israel has strategic importance, as well, as an ally in the case of conflict in the Middle East.

of a buffer between China and Siberia was one of the principal reasons for violent clashes in the 1960s between Chinese
and Soviet troops.

Two views about Russia have emerged: (1) despite political instability, it is in the concert of responsible nations, and
(2) it has no serious intentions of expanding out of northern
Eurasia. For that reason the United States will be reluctant
to challenge Russia if it undertakes to restore at least a sem-
blance of the traditional hegemony of the Russian empire
under the Romanoffs prior to the Communist revolution
of 1917. Not only would it be extremely difficult to project
American force into the interior of Eurasia, but a Russian
sphere of influence over the successor states of the former
Soviet Union might create a more stable region militarily,
economically, and politically.[13]

The United States also will be reluctant to enter into
conflicts in Africa, unless a major outside power tries to gain
control of a region, as was the case with Soviet incursions
during the Cold War, or unless one power attempts to corral
the supply of vital minerals such as cobalt, chromium, or
manganese. Without such incursions, African conflicts constitute little international danger because the continent does
not possess enough inherent military or economic power to
threaten the world. That is why the United States has ignored, militarily at least, the civil wars or ethnic conflicts in
Rwanda, Liberia, Chad, Mozambique, Sudan, and elsewhere. It intervened in Somalia primarily to halt starvation.

The same cannot be said for possible challenges in the

13. Russian hegemony in northern Eurasia is similar in concept to American hegemony over the Western Hemisphere. Neither power can tolerate
the rise of competing states in its region because such states would threaten
its security and prosperity.

Western Hemisphere. The United States will not tolerate any competing power or any great international political movement on either continent. It barely accepted the existence of Communist Cuba and Nicaragua while the Cold War was on, and, as Communism collapses in Cuba, will prevent presence of a Eurasian power there and elsewhere in the hemisphere. Despite ousting a dictator in Haiti and opposing disorder in other Latin American countries, it is unlikely the United States will return to its former "gunboat diplomacy," with overhasty occupation of trouble spots, as happened repeatedly in the first third of the century, and occurred again in the Dominican Republic in 1965, in Grenada in 1983, and in Panama in 1989. But it will fight to prevent any war from spreading or any political movement from reaching continental proportions.

The great danger in Latin America is not from ambitious, growing economic and military powers, but from the perennial conflict between the haves and the have-nots throughout the region. Disputes between the rich and the poor have been the leitmotif of Latin politics since the expulsion of the Spanish and Portuguese imperialists early in the nineteenth century. They explain the revolt by Mayan peasants in the Mexican state of Chiapas in 1994 and the long-standing civil war of the Shining Path Maoists in Peru.[14]

But the rich-poor conflict extends over all of Latin America, and may give rise to wars in the future. Traditionally the United States has sided with the conservative—that is to say, wealthy—forces that have dominated Latin governments. The aim has been to restore order, even if this papered over underlying disorder. But suppressing dissidents does

14. For an analysis of the influence of poverty in the Chiapas revolt, see Alma Guillermoprieto, "Zapata's Heirs," *New Yorker*, May 16, 1994, 52.

not attack the fundamental cause of these conflicts, which is
the enormous disparities of wealth. However, the United
States will find it difficult to champion the oppressed poor
against the establishments, for fear it might set off a conti-
nent-wide revolution. This dilemma may cause great difficulty in the future for the United States.[15]

Internecine or internal ethnic, racial, religious, and other
disputes all over the world hold greater dangers than ever
before for outsiders to be drawn in. Social awareness of people everywhere has been heightened by television reports ap-
pearing on CNN and other networks. When conflicts within
a country result in the massacre of innocents or starvation,
especially of children, human sympathy swells and demands
intensify to alleviate the conditions which brought on the
killings and the hunger.

Even so, the United States will be less likely to enter
into disputes not involving essential American economic and
political interests. We learned in Somalia in 1992–94 how
bottomless such a morass can be, despite unselfish motiva-

15. After military leaders, under General Raoul Cédras, overthrew the
elected president of Haiti, Jean-Bertrand Aristide, the United States instituted an oil embargo, then imposed a general trade embargo in May 1994.
When this failed to force out Cédras, the United States invaded Haiti in
September 1994, overthrew his government, reseated Aristide in office,
and escorted Cédras out of the country. Killings and atrocities by police
and army bullies had turned most of the Haitian people against the military regime, and they largely welcomed the Americans. However, the four
or five hundred members of Haiti's elite families (la bourgeoisie) remained
in control of 80 percent of the country's economy. They opposed Aristide
because he identified with the poor, who make up the vast majority of
Haitians. The elite had helped organize the military coup against Aristide.
Haiti's sharp division between the rich and the poor, and the long anti-
democratic pattern this division has generated, are unlikely to be altered
by a temporary occupation of the country by American troops. See Amy
Wilentz, "Letter from Haiti: Lives in the Balance," New Yorker, December
26, 1994–January 2, 1995, 92.

tions to end the anarchy and starvation there. And we avoided direct intervention in the ethnic wars in the former Yugoslavia because American interests were not deeply involved.[16]

Perhaps we have learned from the Vietnam War and no longer are so worried that we will lose influence and damage our prestige if we pull back from confrontations where our interests are not at stake. Until Vietnam we felt otherwise. General Maxwell Taylor, American ambassador to South Vietnam, told President Lyndon B. Johnson on September 7, 1964: "If we leave Vietnam with our tail between our legs, the consequences of this defeat in the rest of Asia, Africa, and Latin America would be disastrous."[17]

The United States and other nations may find themselves impelled into wars to save disorderly peoples from themselves, but—if the United States is to prevent future Vietnams—it will limit these incursions and get out as quickly as possible. Fortunately, the American romance with "nation-building" is waning and hopefully will fade away. The

16. The greatest single mistake the United States made was to set up an arms embargo which prevented the Bosnian Moslems from arming themselves to fight Serbians, who got weapons from the former Yugoslav army. This stacked the deck against the Moslems and contributed to the killings in the civil war in Bosnia in 1993–94. For an analysis, see Albert Wohlstetter, "Arms, Not Words, for Bosnia," *Wall Street Journal,* May 12, 1994, A14. Active U.S. military response was limited to air strikes against aggressive Serbians carried out through the North Atlantic Treaty Organization (NATO). These were spawned by public revulsion over Serbian massacres of Bosnian Moslems in Sarajevo and other besieged cities. In deciding to respond directly in Bosnia, the Clinton administration reacted more to continuous televised scenes of destruction and death than to national interest. The carnage in Rwanda in the spring of 1994 was much more extensive, but the killings happened quickly and without extensive televised coverage. Consequently, there were few calls for American intervention.

17. Karnow, 399.

United States failed to build a viable nation in South Vietnam despite enormous expense and sacrifice. After the Clinton administration posed nation-building as a goal in Somalia in 1993, there was an outcry from all segments of society.

Critics pointed out anew what should have been self-evident: nations evolve from internal forces and needs; nations cannot be manufactured by outside agencies, using outside standards and practices, and imposed by outsiders on a people or a territory. There remains a hard core of individuals in and out of American government who would like to "build" other nations in the image of the United States. And promoting democracy remains a pillar of U.S. security policy. But the Somalis showed emphatically that they didn't want foreigners trying to build their nation. This forceful, logical stand discredited nation-building with the majority of Americans.

T W O

What Kind of Wars Will We Fight?

I N THIS NEW WORLD, the United States occupies a unique position. As the sole remaining military superpower, the United States possesses more, and more deadly, military hardware than can be brought against it. Laser, radar, infrared, and other sounding devices, plus navigation by satellites orbiting the earth, insure that American defensive weapons can locate and dismantle most enemy control and aiming systems with great speed and that American offensive weapons can be placed precisely on targets.[1]

---

1. In 1990 Colonel David Shaver calculated that U.S. forces had at least a three-to-one edge in combat power over every other country on earth, except the Soviet Union and China. The United States could not "overwhelm" either of these two powers, "nor can either or both overwhelm us," Shaver said. In other words, in a direct confrontation, stalemate would result. Shaver compared tanks, aircraft, combat ships, and army populations, and did not analyze the internal composition of various military forces. However, American weapons and equipment are the most advanced in the world, thereby tending to increase the relative edge of the United States. See Colonel Harry E. Rothmann, unpublished manuscript, "The U.S. Army, Strategic Formulation, and Force Planning: Past, Present, Future" (Newport, R.I.: Naval War College, 1990), 286–88.

Much sophisticated weaponry is being produced in other countries, and potential enemies of the United States, of course, can purchase it. But, with the dismantling of the Soviet military machine, no country has equipment that can challenge overall American superiority. No country is likely to develop such equipment because of the tremendous expense and because such development would send that country on a collision course with the United States long before it could attain parity. An arms race like the one leading up to World War I can't be ruled out, but it's highly improbable.

Although the United States will not face a head-to-head military confrontation against an enemy approaching its strength, Americans should not become complacent and assume we will win any war we enter. Our military superiority alone will not solve our conflicts with other countries. Indeed, we can be led into overconfidence and potential disaster if we rely on such superiority. Other countries can challenge us effectively by fighting indirectly, moving away from our military strength and avoiding large concentrations of weapons and men that we can locate and destroy. Saddam Hussein did not understand this danger, massed his army in and around Kuwait in 1991, and offered a target our guns, aircraft, and missiles could scarcely miss. Few leaders will make this mistake in the future.

In the years ahead, the United States will not lack opponents, and some are certain to be quite capable.

All countries are going to seek their own interests and collide with other powers if they do not achieve them. This does not mean that they necessarily will be aggressive or seeking to achieve hegemony over a region. For example, in a 1993 book which identifies the United States as China's principal military adversary, Chinese military leaders and academic allies quoted President Jiang Zemin as saying, "We must win high-tech, small-scale wars under modern conditions." This implies that China would choose arenas where it could avoid a direct challenge to the American behemoth and force it to engage on terms favorable to China. The book mentioned eight possible war scenarios, including retaking Taiwan, fighting another war in Korea, and seizure of oil fields that China claims in the South China Sea.[2]

These potential conflicts reflect three of China's principal concerns, all related to security and economic advancement. But the book speaks of worst-case situations, and the government quickly withdrew the statement. None aims at regional hegemony, and none reflects opposition to the United States. However, each illustrates a type of quarrel that can disturb the peace.

Another question would be raised if Japan struck a deal with Russia to exploit the forest and mineral resources of Siberia in return for assisting Russia's industry and training its workers. Japan contemplated joining Germany in its 1941 attack against the Soviet Union in order to get these raw materials. The United States would find it difficult to oppose a Japan-Russia commercial arrangement, even though it would strengthen Japan immensely.

These possible scenarios raise the question of precisely what situations would cause the United States to undertake a major force projection beyond its territory.

Sometimes the issue is clear: if North Korea attempted to conquer South Korea again, the United States would protect its ally. So long as the United States did not attempt to

2. "Chinese Book Offers Eight War Scenarios in which America Is Principal Adversary," (New York *Times* Service), Richmond *Times-Dispatch*, November 17, 1993, A4.

conquer North Korea, China would not intervene, just as it didn't intervene in the Korean War until it realized American troops were marching toward the Yalu River opposite its frontier, thereby threatening to eliminate China's historic buffer. For a thousand years Korea had been a shield for China against incursions from the sea.[3]

But what should be the American response if China finally decided to take over Taiwan? Both the Communists on the mainland and the Nationalists on Taiwan agree that the island is merely a province of China. Of course, it served for a generation as a forward American bastion against Red China, when American leaders were convinced China entertained aggressive ideas in East Asia. These ideas were false, but the attitude lingers on.[4] Chinese repossession of Taiwan would not imply that Beijing was seeking hegemony over East Asia, only that it was achieving unification. The United States would not complain if the island reunited peacefully with China. But, such is the impact of emotions and of old antagonisms, strong voices would be raised in the United States to resist if the Red Chinese tried to seize Taiwan by force.

If Japan attempted to overawe China again, its purpose would be to achieve regional hegemony, as was its aim from the Sino-Japanese War of 1894–95 through World War II.

3. Some observers believe China would not object to the destruction of North Korea, since this unreconstructed, trigger-happy state with nuclear pretensions is a thorn in the flesh of all East Asia. However, China most probably would demand a unified Korea that was unaligned. China leaders still remember that this peninsula, while under the domination of Japan, was the springboard for Japanese aggression against China for decades. It would be extremely suspicious of a Korea tied to the United States.

4. For an analysis of American misconceptions about Taiwan, see Bevin Alexander, *The Strange Connection: American Intervention in China, 1944–72* (Westport, Ct.: Greenwood Press, 1992).

Such a move would signal aggressive intent and an aspiration to recreate something akin to Japan's exploitative but still-born "Greater East Asia Co-Prosperity Sphere" of 1940. Therefore, the United States should join with China, Korea, and, perhaps, Russia, to stop such an effort.

Similarly, the United States would be forced to resist if Russia attacked Iran and recommenced its drive to the Persian Gulf—an aspiration that Imperial Britain aborted in the nineteenth century in what came to be known as "The Great Game." Such a move would destabilize Asia, threaten India and Pakistan, and deliver a large part of the world's oil into Russia's hands.

But there are innumerable other possible scenarios in which American interests would not be so self-evident. What if Turkey and Greece went to war over possession of Cyprus? What if Bulgaria and Serbia started fighting over Macedonia? Or Romania and Hungary over Transylvania? What if India and Pakistan collided again over Kashmir?

It's pointless to list all the possible danger points between countries and within countries. What's clear is that the ones that will draw in the United States will occur mostly around the periphery of Eurasia, to prevent the rise of a regional or continental hegemonic power that can build a world navy; in Africa to deter a power from cornering the market in a vital mineral, or in Latin America, to prevent a power or a political movement from threatening U.S. control of the Western Hemisphere.

As reflected in Jiang Zemin's reference to "small-scale wars," the United States most probably will face opponents who conduct comparatively limited conflicts, such as those by the Chinese in Korea 1950–53 and the Communists in Vietnam in the 1960s and early 1970s. In both cases, our enemies did not challenge our weapons' superiority, but came in "under" American technology, refusing to confront it directly, but nevertheless presenting a great challenge to American arms.

In Korea, the Chinese fought largely in high mountains where American armor and motorized equipment were not decisive. They dug deep bunkers and covered them with heavy timbers, earth, and rocks, making them virtually impervious to air attacks and artillery. The Chinese brought reinforcements, food, ammunition and other supplies forward at night, reducing interdiction by American air power. They fought largely with rifles, machine guns, hand grenades and mortars. These weapons and ammunition for them could be carried on the backs of porters, avoiding roads and the necessity of using trucks. In order to defeat the Chinese, the Americans had to meet them on their own terms—climbing the steep ridgelines and driving them out of their bunkers in bloody, close engagements fought almost hand-to-hand. The cost of these battles was so great that the United States elected to make peace rather than drive the Chinese out of Korea.

In Vietnam the Communists waged primarily a guerrilla war. During the period of American involvement, they broke this rule only twice: when major U.S. forces deployed in 1965–66 and in the Tet offensive of 1968. In both instances, the Communists challenged American power directly, but suffered tremendous losses. They reverted to small-unit skirmishes, in which American power could not be brought to bear in overwhelming strength. The North Vietnamese and Vietcong largely refused to meet Americans in face-to-face confrontations where U.S. firepower could be decisive. Instead, they used the region's tropical forests, mountains, rivers, and farmland to camouflage small but damaging hit-and-run strikes by soldiers who emerged from and melted back at will into the forests or the largely friendly population, rendering them extremely hard to find. They maintained no battle lines, and made no distinction between their own and enemy territory. After the withdrawal of American forces, they won the war in 1975 with conventional forces deployed in conventional ways against South Vietnamese units which had largely lost their resolve.

In the Persian Gulf War of 1991, Iraq tried the reverse of guerrilla strategy: confronting American weaponry on even terms. It suffered overwhelming defeat. Though it possessed many expensive weapons and had invested heavily in training a modern military force, Iraq was virtually helpless against the United States because its technology, though advanced, remained inferior to American technology. A force armed with inferior weapons that directly opposes a force deploying superior weapons will nearly always be destroyed.

This was how, for example, at Omdurman in the Sudan in 1898, British General Sir Horatio Kitchener was able to defeat a huge army of Mahdi dervishes. Rudyard Kipling immortalized the "Fuzzy-Wuzzy" as "a pore benighted 'eathen but a first-class fightin' man," yet the dervishes—armed largely with swords and spears—were no match for Kitchener's twenty machine guns. The Madhi lost 10,000 men and an equal number were wounded or captured, compared to minimal British casualties.

The United States can anticipate that the enemies it meets in the future who adopt the policies of the Chinese in the Korean War or the Communists in the Vietnam War will be difficult to defeat, whereas powers that have good weaponry but remain technologically inferior to the United States are likely to be destroyed in short order if they try to confront American forces on even terms.

However, it is important for the American political leadership to have a clear idea of what it wishes to achieve against any enemy. As pointed out by retired Vice Admiral Gerald E. Miller—who commanded a division of aircraft carriers off Vietnam during the war—the U.S. political leadership tied the hands of the military in Vietnam. "The leadership somehow got the impression that we could win a military conflict by air power," Miller said. "We remained on the defensive, thinking that air power alone could destroy the logistic train and demoralize the opposition. That was a political wish, not a sound military strategy."[5] Victory comes from human beings moving into enemy territory and taking charge.

The civilian leadership in Washington concluded that the North Vietnamese would quit in the face of overwhelming American power, and refused to accept any professional opinion to the contrary.[6]

The government designed its rules of engagement in Vietnam to prevent the entry of the Chinese into the war, as had happened in Korea. The U.S. government knew the threat of Chinese intervention in Vietnam was real, because the Chinese had made plain at the 1954 Geneva conference and afterward that any attempt by the United States to eliminate North Vietnam as a buffer on their southern frontier would result in Chinese intervention.

The tragedy is that the political leaders of the United States did not see that avoiding the invasion of North Viet-

5. Letter from retired Vice Admiral Gerald E. Miller to author, November 29, 1993.

6. Letter from retired Rear Admiral Clarence A. Hill, Jr. to author, November 29, 1993.

nam, plus allowing Chinese and Soviet arms to go into North Vietnam unhindered, compromised the American position in Vietnam fatally and forced the military to pursue a war it should not have been called upon to fight.

The political inhibitions we built into the conflict led directly to the military impasse. The government refused to own up to these contradictions. Instead, it ordered the military to go in and win, meanwhile imposing conditions that made victory impossible.

Politicans find it easy to justify their interference in military affairs. Not only does the U.S. Constitution name the president as the commander in chief, but politicians are given to quoting Georges Clemenceau, World War I French premier, who said "wars are too important to be left to the generals." Similarly, the most-remembered line of the nineteenth-century Prussian military theorist, Karl von Clausewitz, is that "war is a mere continuation of policy by other means."

However, long before we took notice of Clausewitz or Clemenceau, Americans had come to a bizarre conclusion about warfare. Possibly because of our arrogance that it was our "manifest destiny" to expand across the North American continent, and possibly because we encountered weak Native American tribes that could not be assimilated into our culture, we developed the theory that we should attain total victory over our opponents. President Franklin D. Roosevelt codified the concept in World War II by proclaiming that the Allies would only accept "unconditional surrender" from the Axis powers. The belief attained canonical form when General Douglas MacArthur told the 1962 West Point graduating class: "Your mission remains fixed, determined, inviolable. It is to win our wars. . . . In war, there is no substitute for victory." On frequent occasions since, MacArthur's statement has been cited as an axiom, as a principle upon which our nation must base its military aspirations.

Yet it is a patent falsehood. Except for our wars against Native Americans, only one major American conflict ended in total surrender of the enemy: the Civil War. And in that war we actually both won and lost, since part of our people defeated the other part. Even in World War II, we did not entirely adhere to unconditional surrender. We applied the rule only to Nazi Germany, a decision that strengthened Adolf Hitler's hold on the German people and forced them to struggle on much longer than they might if they had been offered a way out. Realizing that the Japanese would fight to the bitter end unless they kept their emperor, we relented and even allowed them to retain the very government that had warred against us. The Japanese never had their national ethics, identity, or sense of cohesion called into question. This decision made American occupation of Japan infinitely easier and led to speedy reconciliation of the United States and Japan.

We frequently forget it in the heat of an international crisis, but the actual purpose of war, as Clausewitz stated, is to achieve our political aims. Victory in war is only a means to that end. If our aims can be attained without force, or by settling for less than complete victory, our purpose is achieved. The job of the American military is not to win wars, as MacArthur insisted, but to gain our political purposes. Military victory, in this context, is irrelevant. It is only relevant if it leads to gaining our political ends.

A political solution resulting in a more perfect peace is nearly always the goal. This is best accomplished, not by war, but by looking hard at our nation's real needs and our antagonist's actual motivations and seeking a resolution through negotiation. An objective, dispassionate look at Vietnam would have shown that the people were absorbed in a civil war and had no interest in conquering the rest of Southeast Asia for the Kremlin. The "falling-domino theory" was a nightmare without substance. However, leaders often fail to ascertain their country's real purposes. In times of stress or fear they usually are driven by passions, not reason, and react with anger or bellicosity to challenges.

As a consequence, politicians as a rule do not face up to the military implications of their political decisions. This led in Vietnam to American leaders imposing political burdens that made it impossible for the armed forces to fight the battles and campaigns necessary to win. Politicians should set forth the actual aims of a conflict, in order for the military to determine whether these aims can be met within the framework of the political limitations imposed. If they can't, we should either change the aims or get out. But it's doubtful whether politicians can be so honest, especially if high political stakes are involved.

Furthermore, military leaders cannot be relied on to be more objective than political leaders. The sad truth about the Vietnam War is that the nation's top military brass were willing victims of the politicians' desires. They did not study the conditions imposed by the civilian leadership in sufficient depth to conclude that the war was unwinnable. Rather, they went along eagerly with the political leaders in the commitment of American forces. They believed that the Vietcong insurgency could be destroyed by bombing North Vietnam and by challenging North Vietnamese regular forces to battle where U.S. firepower would overwhelm them.

This, they thought, would leave the South Vietnamese

government and its military forces free to eradicate Communist infrastructures in the villages. But the South Vietnamese were not capable of destroying the Vietcong on their own, and the North Vietnamese were largely successful in drawing American ground forces away from the populated regions into mountains and jungles along the frontiers. There the Communists fought only when, where and how long they wanted, withdrawing into "neutral" Laos or Cambodia whenever pressure mounted. Since American policy for most of the war prohibited American hot pursuit into these countries, the North Vietnamese possessed a sanctuary fully as useful as its sanctuary in North Vietnam itself.[7] The brass thereby contributed to the disaster.

The sober lesson: if political and military leaders fail to confront reality, future Vietnams are possible.

Since there is no Soviet Union or other major power with a huge modern military machine, the United States is unlikely to face a great power-against-power, direct, sweeping military challenge, such as it met in World War II. The United States and other countries most likely will encounter comparative "little" wars that have specific, relatively limited objectives. The U.S. military calls them "low-intensity conflicts" or LICs.

Two distinct types of LICs are possible: (1) wars to oppose aggression, such as the United States and its allies fought against Iraq in 1991, and (2) essentially guerrilla wars characterized by indirection, subterfuge, and circuitous ap-

---

7. For an analysis of the support of the American military leadership in the commitment to Vietnam, see Krepinevich, 140–52. Regarding the anger of American fighting men at being confronted with the Cambodian sanctuary, see Moore and Galloway, 341.

proaches, such as the Communists fought against the United States in Vietnam 1965–73.

The United States will fight few LICs against aggressors who invade another country. Such wars will have predictable outcomes, since any country invading a state the United States considers important to protect is almost certain to crumple against American military power. The situation is not so clear cut for guerrilla-type LICs. Guerrillas strike primarily by ambush against the weaknesses of conventional forces—lines of communication and supply, rear bases, cities, convoys, and isolated outposts. In such wars, superior weapons are to a large degree neutralized. Will is the determining factor.

But there is one element in all guerrilla operations that fundamentally limits their application: they are great for defensive wars but useless for aggressive wars.

This is because guerrilla forces utterly depend upon the goodwill and support of the people. The essential difference of guerrilla war from conventional war is that guerrillas don't maintain a battle line or "main line of resistance." Guerrillas operate in the rear of the enemy and must rely upon a friendly population to feed, support, and, sometimes, hide them. This means that guerrilla warfare can only succeed in one's own country. An aggressor invading another country cannot fight a guerrilla war because the people are certain to be hostile.

Thus, any country that invades another country must fight a conventional war. If the United States decides to thwart that aggressor it can do so, because its conventional war strength far surpasses that of any other state. Even if the United States decides not to assist, the invaded country by no means must surrender, though its military forces might be woefully inferior to the invader's. It can move to guerrilla war and prevent the invader from achieving victory. It may take time and will be costly, but the history of such wars in this century demonstrates that guerrillas can create a stalemate. In time, an invader will withdraw rather than endure the slow bloodletting and heavy expenditures that a stand-off produces.

But this rule also applies to the United States: it likewise cannot conduct an aggressive war, except against a country, like Panama in 1989, that largely welcomes intervention because of unsatisfactory internal conditions. This will disturb Americans who clamor for a decisive "Shootout at the OK Corral" with a particularly obnoxious country. But it will force politicians and military leaders, who may want to lead the United States into an aggressive military adventure, to consider their choices realistically.

In summary, the United States will be able to win LICs in friendly countries invaded by another power, but it will run a severe risk of generating a guerrilla war and a military stalemate if it invades another country, however weak. Since leaders everywhere were made aware of U.S. military power in the Gulf War, few countries will challenge the United States by invading another country, as Saddam Hussein did. If an irreconcilable crisis comes with the United States, a power most probably will try to induce American forces to invade its territory, thereby securing the support of its people and access to the great potential advantage of irregular or guerrilla warfare.

This kind of war is the greatest trap, especially since American politicians have a tendency to intervene in countries that offend them or where they see strategic dangers. Unfortunately, we sometimes get enmeshed and remain for years. We are still in South Korea, forty-five years after the Korean War started. We protected Taiwan against Red China for a generation, and were involved in South Vietnam directly or indirectly for twenty years.

A firefight of U.S. forces with clansmen in Somalia in 1993 offered a preview at an elementary level of what advanced forces can encounter when they invade even the weakest country. Eighteen Americans were killed and eighty-four wounded on October 3, 1993, in an ambush of a U.S. Army Ranger detachment in the capital, Mogadishu. The Defense Department had denied offensive armor, like tanks and Bradley fighting vehicles, to forces in Somalia, seeing the American role as peacekeeping, not battle. The officer in charge of the raid, Major General William Garrison, said few losses would have been avoided if armor had been provided. However, armored vehicles might have forced their way through Somali roadblocks and deflected rifle and machine gun fire. Yet it's true that a determined enemy operating in the close quarters of a city in turmoil, as Mogadishu was in 1993, may have opportunities to approach American armored vehicles and destroy them with relatively unsophisticated weapons.[8]

For example, Somalis firing hand-held launchers from cover knocked down American helicopters with rocket grenades. Afghan rebels did the same against Soviet helicopters using American-supplied Stinger missiles. In the Korean War, American forces, wielding an improved "bazooka," or antitank rocket, were able to get close to and destroy numerous North Korean T34 tanks that made the mistake of ad-

8. General Garrison made his appraisal before the Senate Armed Services Committee on May 12, 1994. See Associated Press article, "Clinton: Ill-fated raid was a surprise," Richmond *Times-Dispatch,* May 13, 1994, A20.

vancing into the closely built city of Taejon. Later in the war, Chinese soldiers dismantled some American tanks by approaching them unobserved at night or in towns and planting satchel charges of high explosives under them.

Outstanding guerrilla leaders in this century developed sophisticated and effective principles on how to combat more powerful forces. Their lessons remain highly pertinent, because most wars in the future are likely to exploit these principles. In later chapters we will examine how these great guerrilla leaders operated.

The American military cannot abandon its large inventory of advanced weapons designed for larger wars on the theory that only smaller, limited wars will be fought. Nor can it cease developing weapons or defenses against weapons. A potential enemy is likely to create the weaponry or defenses to exploit any gap that the United States allows to occur in its arsenal.

At the Army War College's 1994 strategy conference, Dr. John F. Guilmartin, Jr., an expert on weapons, said: "Our lead in high tech is safe, but bad guys can do much in a number of fields." He mentioned electromagnetic pulses, which might be unleashed by an enemy over a wide area. These have the potential of knocking out electronics, and neutralizing the computers which drive American detection and weapons systems. He also pointed out that the Americans had a difficult time finding the moveable Scud missiles the Iraqis employed in the Persian Gulf War—and that mobile missile technology can be developed further. Guilmartin mentioned as other potentially dangerous technological innovations: stealth cruise missiles, gases, bacterial diseases, and nonacute infections to affect vision or cause arthritis or other ailments that might be spread among an enemy population.

In a similar vein, the futurists Alvin and Heidi Toffler in *War and Anti-War* postulate weapons that stun or incapacitate people without actually killing them.

One of the greatest dangers is further development of stealth technology. A key factor in U.S. military superiority is the ability of detection systems to locate enemy weapons, often at night and often when they are camouflaged. The American stealth bomber uses advanced materials and technology to reduce the reflection of radio beams from its surface, thereby hiding the bomber's presence from radar. Further development along this line might permit other weapons to hide from radar, infrared, sonar, and other detection devices. This would make enemy forces less visible and offer immense scope to a strategy designed to avoid challenging American power directly but rather striking at U.S. forces "stealthily" by ambushes and surprise attacks.

Consequently, the United States must continue its research and development of weapons and counterweapons. Also, it can reduce the numbers of some of its weapons but cannot give up the wide assortment that makes the United States formidable in any environment and against any type of resistance. For example, the army cannot abandon tanks on the premise that it is most likely in the future to encounter guerrilla or semiguerrilla wars, such as it fought in Vietnam, and these wars are most likely to be conducted by lightly armed soldiers in jungles, forests, flooded rice paddies, or high mountains where tanks have limited usefulness. Not only can semiguerrilla wars also be fought in open terrain, such as Somalia, where armor does have a role, but tanks and weapons to kill tanks (like the shoulder-mounted Javelin missile) must be on hand in the event any other power decides to use armor.

The first weeks of the Korean War offer an example of the sort of danger that can occur when a particular enemy weapon cannot be countered. The North Koreans deployed only 150 Soviet T34 tanks, but they were able to advance almost unmolested in the first days of the war because—until American antitank weapons could be rushed in—the South Koreans had nothing that could counter the T34, neither antitank rockets, napalm, land mines, nor antitank artillery rounds.

The U.S. military must prepare for any contingency. This means that the military must have a ready basket or "toolbox" of flexible, general-purpose forces and weapons with the capability of responding to a number of challenges and performing a range of operations it might be called upon to undertake—even though Americans are likely to fight low-intensity wars mainly against guerrillas or semiguerrillas.

A policy of broad preparation will provide insurance in the event that a conflict develops which no one anticipated. For example, the United States is extremely unlikely to fight Russia, but such a war cannot be ruled out. There is a strong, and understandable, urge in the military to possess as wide a range of capabilities as possible, in order to insure having forces that are "not too badly wrong," because no one can ever predict future challenges precisely and thus always "have it right." This is not as daunting a problem as it may appear. U.S. Army Colonel Harry E. Rothmann of the National War College points out that perhaps 80 percent of the tasks an army must perform are common to any scenario it might encounter. It's the other 20 percent that units or detachments must be specifically trained to perform.[9]

The Defense Department's "Bottom-up Review," issued in 1993 by Les Aspin, secretary of defense, institutionalized the concept of being "not too badly wrong." Aspin expressed the idea in a positive way by calling for the United States to be prepared to fight two "major regional conflicts" at the same time. But he cited no specific threats and used an attack by Iraq on Kuwait and Saudi Arabia and by North Korea against South Korea as examples of the types of possible conflicts he envisioned. The two regional conflicts concept is really a smokescreen. The plan actually calls for the United States to have sufficient force to fight any likely challenger anywhere. Also Aspin wrote: "History suggests that we most often deter the conflicts that we plan for and actually fight the ones we do not anticipate." Aspin expected to get forces for "peace enforcement and intervention operations"—that is, future Somalias—from general-purpose units collected to fight regional conflicts.

Aspin's major innovation was to renew the call made by President George Bush's secretary of defense, Dick Cheney, for improving capacity to lift forces quickly to trouble spots by air and by sea. He also accepted the necessity of continued development of weapons in order to "maintain the technological superiority of our weapons and equipment."[10]

9. Colonels Bruce Harris, George Raach, Harry Rothmann, James Stefan, Jim Smith, David Wilson, Dave Tretler. Interview by author September 29, 1993, with faculty, Department of Military Strategy and Operations, National War College, Fort McNair, Washington, D.C.

10. Les Aspin, "The Bottom-up Review: Forces for a New Era" (Washington, D.C.: Department of Defense), September 1, 1993.

THREE

America Rules
the Waves

THERE ARE TWO ELEMENTS affecting the future of warfare that relate specifically to the fact that nearly three-quarters of the earth are covered by oceans.

The first is that it is upon the oceans that the vast bulk of the oil, textiles, food, machinery, and other manufactured products in overseas exchange are carried. Since trade is the principal concern of all nations, the United States is the most important factor in determining whether the world will remain open to trade or succumb to protectionism. This is not because the United States has the world's largest economy but because it possesses the world's greatest navy.

The second element is that the U.S. Navy, primarily by means of carrier task forces, can project power to any coast on earth where the nation decides it must gain control. There it can blockade an enemy's ports or, with the air force, form a shield for army or marine forces to invade.

The United States also is the only power that can exert the necessary force to stop any other state from projecting a major military operation by sea to a distant shore, or to promote or prevent trade. As the classic definer of sea power, Alfred Thayer Mahan, pointed out a century ago, the greatest navy can sweep the navies—and the commerce—of all other countries from the seas.

The U.S. Navy advertises that it has adopted a new strategy of concentrating on maneuver from the sea and warfare around the littorals (coastal regions) of the world's oceans. This change, the navy says, "represents a fundamental shift away from open-ocean warfighting on the sea toward joint operations conducted from the sea."[1] However, no navy—including that of the Soviet Union—has challenged American control of the open oceans since the U.S. Navy destroyed Japan's last fleet off the Philippines in 1944. Since World War II, all naval military actions have been maneuvers or threats onto the littoral "from the sea": Korea, Quemoy and Matsu islands off China, Vietnam, Lebanon, and the Persian Gulf War, plus many smaller force projections.

The great military advantage of carrier task forces is that they permit the United States to make its power felt on any shore where ships can sail and on the hinterland behind that shore. Since the major potential dangers to the United States are countries with seacoasts, carriers are always a latent threat. The navy can physically reach almost any spot in the world where it may have to exert its force. Once there, it can establish a virtually permanent presence. The navy also permits the United States to maintain its military superiority, because by controlling the seas, it can assure seaborne delivery of American ground forces wherever they have to be sent.

As discussed in chapter 1, the U.S. Navy finds itself now with the same capability the Royal Navy possessed from the

---

1. U.S. Navy and Marine Corps White Paper, ". . . From the Sea," 1993, 3.

seventeenth century through World War I. In that era the
Royal Navy exploited its command of the seas by insuring
that world trade would flow on terms advantageous to Britain. Any country that challenged Britain suffered the destruction not only of its navy but of its seaborne commerce.
In this period Holland, Spain, and France contested Britain
and, losing, endured enormous economic damage. Britain
succeeded because it had the most men-of-war and the best
seamen and because it acquired colonies or safe ports at the
ends of trade routes. There its ships, military and merchant,
could lie in safety.

Today such bases are no longer necessary. The U.S.
Navy's *Nimitz*-class nuclear-powered aircraft carriers can go
one million miles without refueling. Though support ships
have shorter ranges and may have to be resupplied with fuel
or replaced on long voyages, an eight-to-twelve-ship American carrier task force can project enormous power wherever
the ocean rolls.

Moreover, forward-deployed carriers can reach a danger
spot faster than any other major force. When Iraq invaded
Kuwait on August 2, 1990, the nuclear carrier *Eisenhower* was
at Naples, Italy, and the nonnuclear carrier *Independence* was
in the eastern Indian Ocean. Within forty-eight hours these
ships were at points within range of Iraqi targets. This may
have played some role in stopping Iraq from marching into
Saudi Arabia.[2]

In addition, a carrier task force at sea is extremely hard to
hit. This is despite the doubts raised about the survivability
of warships after an Argentine airplane destroyed the Royal
Navy's most modern vessel, HMS *Sheffield*, with a single

2. *Sea Power*, September 1993, 29.

French-made Exocet missile in the Falklands War of 1982. The *Sheffield* did not possess enough defensive weapons to ward off a missile attack, whereas a carrier task force has an immense array of guns, missiles, and aerial platforms that can stop practically any missile, aircraft, or submarine thrown against it.[3]

A task force's first line of defense consists of specially designed early-warning aircraft, operating two-hundred or more miles from the force. These aircraft detect air and surface objects, including incoming missiles, and can direct U.S. aircraft or weapons to destroy missiles or attackers. Backing up these early-warning aircraft are nuclear-powered attack submarines and antisubmarine fixed-wing aircraft with sensors and weapons to destroy enemy subs. Closer in to the force are antisubmarine helicopters working with surface escorts with antiair and antisub weapons. Consequently, a task force can detect, identify, locate, and destroy an enemy threat well before it can reach the core of the force, the carrier.

There have been suggestions that jet-propelled cruise missiles on the order of American Tomahawks could replace aircraft carriers. Tomahawks can be dispatched at ranges of more than 500 miles, can get under enemy radar by flying as close as fifty feet to the surface, and can confuse defenders by following evasive flight paths. Naval ships launched them with great effect against targets on shore during the Gulf War. They also can be fired against other ships, giving rise to the argument that they may be a less-vulnerable substitute for a carrier task force. But cruise missiles, even guided by inerrant satellite navigation, will have great difficulty hitting

3. Interview by author with U. S. Navy retired admirals Thomas H. Moorer, C. A. Hill, Jr., William P. Lawrence, Gerald E. Miller, and M. W. Cagle, September 30, 1993, Arlington, Virginia.

ships at sea. Ships are constantly moving, whereas a cruise missile, to be deadly accurate, must be plotted against a stationary target. Also, cruise missile aiming radar cannot distinguish the size of a ship, seeing a small vessel and the heart of a task force, the carrier, as the same. In addition, sophisticated defense systems such as a carrier task force deploys can detect and destroy most cruise missiles. Finally, present-day cruise missiles carry only about a thousand pounds of payload.[4]

By comparison, a nuclear carrier mounts eighty-five to ninety aircraft and these can fly 100 to 150 sorties a day, around the clock, for weeks at a time. About half will be defensive sorties to protect the carrier group, the other half attack strikes by upgraded F-14s and F / A-18s.[5] But the F-14 can carry four tons of payload (plus four air-to-air missiles) and the F / A-18 8.5 tons. These aircraft can deliver about 450 tons of ordnance in a day—or the equivalent of 900 Tomahawks.[6] Although cruise missiles are important offensive weapons, they cannot produce the enormous concentrated striking power of a carrier task force.

The U.S. Air Force can use overseas land bases outside of

4. I am indebted to retired Vice Admirals Gerald E. Miller and M. W. Cagle for this description of the defense capabilities of carrier task forces and their superiority over cruise missiles.

5. A-6s will not be flown off carriers after about 1995 or 1996.

6. Friedman and Lebard, 229. Carrier-borne attack aircraft and bombers are more versatile than land-based long-range bombers, which are limited to only a few missions. For example, air force B-52 bombers were employed almost solely against troop concentrations in the Vietnam War and Persian Gulf War. Carrier aircraft can perform many missions, including attacks against troops, interdiction of supply lines, anti-air and anti-submarine warfare, close support of U. S. combat forces, electronic countermeasures, and amphibious warfare. See Vice Admiral William P. Lawrence (retired), "Can Land-Based Bombers Replace Aircraft Carriers?" *Naval Institute Proceedings,* June 1993, 12–13.

immediate combat areas to mount air strikes at potential danger spots. From such bases (like those in Turkey in the Persian Gulf War), air force stealth aircraft and increased-range aircraft should reduce air losses from ground attacks dramatically. However, aircraft at fixed forward bases within a combat area tend to be more vulnerable. The United States does not have enough overseas land bases to mount air strikes at all potential danger spots, and may not get enough of them in the future. In the Vietnam War, more than 400 U.S. and allied aircraft were lost from ground attacks and more than 4,000 additional were damaged. But, since North Vietnamese aircraft could not reach the carriers, not a single sea-based aircraft was lost or damaged on them.[7]

The navy has a weakness as well: controlling close-in approaches to land and choke points. Retired Vice Admiral M. W. Cagle says an enemy with few or no ships in some cases can make it difficult to land soldiers or marines on shore in narrow waters by deploying mines, missiles, and submarines. "Today's terrible mines, magnetic, pressure, contact, and with ingenious ways for them to 'count' passing vessels before becoming activated, pose one great problem for us and a smart and inexpensive counter by an opponent."[8]

In summary, the combination of the strengths of all the services can optimize their effects, while offsetting their weaknesses. The air force is the nation's "long arm," capable of swift, devastating strikes from great distances. The navy can project a forward presence on any shoreline. The army can deliver sustained combat, a process that can destroy en-

7. *Sea Power,* September 1993, 34.

8. Letter to author from Admiral Cagle, January 15, 1994.

emy forces. No country in the world can defeat this combination.[9]

It is impossible to predict whether a major Eurasian power will embark, as Germany did twice and Japan once in this century, on a march to gain regional or continental hegemony. History shows that economic problems combined with national avarice can produce the toxic reaction of aggression. However, if the United States maintains its superior military power and if it challenges aggressors the first time they show their nature, aggression may be averted—or stopped in time.

Even without overt aggression by ambitious powers, however, economic issues are so important to people that chances of collisions over them are great. Most nations and groups of nations attempt to exploit economic opportunities wherever they find them and try to carve out domains which favor themselves and discourage or exclude others.[10]

The United States can now dominate the world's economy, if it chooses. As shown in chapter 1, its navy rules the oceans and can order sea-borne trade to its liking, and it can control the oil production and reserves of the Persian Gulf or anywhere else oil is carried by sea. Persian Gulf petroleum, plus that of North America which the United States already controls, equals 35 percent of world oil production and harbors 65 percent of world reserves. Other nations have awakened to the realization that U.S. domination of the Persian

9. Letter to author from Colonel George T. Raach, National War College faculty, December 8, 1993.

10. Bob Davis and Jackie Calmes, "However Nafta Fares, U. S. Is Paring Down Its Trade Leadership," *Wall Street Journal,* November 17, 1993, A1; Lawrence Ingrassia and Bhushan Bahree, "Nafta Victory Keeps GATT's Chances Alive," *Wall Street Journal,* November 19, 1993, A7.

Gulf means it has the power to set production quotas and prices, and direct the movement of oil.[11]

Since any U.S. effort to hold oil and the sea lanes hostage would result in an immense anti-American alliance, the United States is far more likely to use other devices to advance its economic interests. The rise of great regional trading blocs, like the European Union and the North American Free Trade Agreement, arouses the greatest anxiety because they erect barriers against outsiders.

The world is far from achieving economic laissez-faire or unrestricted trade as advocated by Adam Smith in his *Wealth of Nations* in 1776 and ballyhooed by numerous politicians as the goal today. Instead, the world still faces the enormous dangers of protectionism. After World War I numerous governments attempted to restrict trade by seeking autarky, or economic self-sufficiency within their countries or empires and reducing imports from the outside. This not only exacerbated the worldwide economic depression of the 1930s but was one of the causes of World War II.

An expression of this effort was the Smoot-Hawley Tariff Act of 1930, which set the highest import duties in U.S. history, led to retaliation in Europe, reduced world trade greatly, and contributed to an already powerful urge by Japan to carve out an empire in East Asia. American opposition led directly to the Japanese attack on Pearl Harbor in December 1941 and to American entrance into World War II.

Today nearly all national governments realize that the world depends upon international trade and there are strong movements to reduce tariff barriers and other restrictions limiting traffic between countries and blocs of countries. But

11. Friedman and Lebard, 209–211.

history shows that peoples seek their economic advancement, even at the expense of others. Human cupidity will always threaten overt or covert efforts to inhibit trade—and this tendency constitutes a great potential source of war.

One instance of the sorts of problems we will face: cobalt, chromium, platinum, and manganese are essential to some industrial production and cannot be substituted. For example, chromium is required to make alloys hard enough to withstand the high combustion temperatures of gas-turbine engines. Most of the world's cobalt comes from Zaire and Zambia; most of its chromium, platinum, and manganese, vital in some industrial processes, comes from South Africa. Political problems in these countries could hurt all industrial powers. Likewise, efforts to corral supplies of these minerals by the United States or its major industrial competitors, Japan, the European Union, and the Pacific Rim countries, could destabilize the world.[12]

The United States, through military intervention in regions of contention, or through the force of its navy upon the oceans, can restrict world trade to its advantage. The United States is extremely unlikely to exercise this power. It seeks peace and prosperity throughout the world, and will almost assuredly keep world trade relatively open. Nevertheless, protectionist systems such as the European Union and NAFTA leave the question open as to whether there will be a resurrection of efforts at autarkic self-sufficiency.

12. Kent H. Butts, "The Department of Defense Role in African Policy," *Parameters,* U.S. Army War College Quarterly, (Winter 1993–94), 63–64.

FOUR

New Tactics for a New Army

AMERICAN SOLDIERS in future wars will form small battle groups of combined arms. These groups will operate independently but will coordinate with other groups. They will possess high mobility either in land or air vehicles, and will wield weapons that are deadly and accurate at long ranges against enemy weapons and people. They will also possess defenses that will make it difficult for enemies to hit them.

But none of these factors will guarantee victory. This is because the essential challenge in most wars the United States will face will hinge on the resolve or determination of the enemy, not his weapons. Because of this, the United States faces an additional trial besides that of finding ways to counter the armament other countries might deploy.

The Persian Gulf War showed why will rather than weapons constitutes the major test for future conflicts. This conflict demonstrated that merely modern armaments, such as Iraq possessed, were useless against American weapons, which were at the leading edge of technology. One example:

U.S. aircraft, cruise missiles, and attack helicopters, with precision strikes, crippled the Iraqi air-defense and command, control, and communication systems within a few hours after the shooting war started on January 16, 1991. Another example: American F-15C air-superiority fighters shot down thirty-three Iraqi aircraft without a single loss.[1]

As we saw in chapter 2, no other country possesses weapons as powerful and as accurate as American armament, and is not likely to develop them because of the cost and because any such move would invite a preemptive strike by the United States.

Therefore, as we also saw in chapter 2, most countries will avoid invasions of other countries and will attempt to draw us into their own territories. There, despite military inferiority, they can fight a guerrilla or semi-guerrilla war and take advantage of the sympathy and assistance of their own people.

Although a defensive war fought in an enemy's own land represents the greatest U.S. challenge, most military theoretical thought has been directed at tactical and strategic problems we would face in an aggressive war against a power equal to us in weapons and technology. The American military spent forty-five years pondering such a war because of the danger from the Soviet Union, so it's no wonder analysts have focused on an evenly matched clash between Titans.

Some recent thinking, however, has application to any fight we might enter, including low-intensity conflicts. A few U.S. Army theoreticians believe the army's present emphasis on massive firepower and use of maneuver forces mounted on armored vehicles like tanks and armored personnel carri-

1. *Conduct of the Persian Gulf War,* 114–22; 692–93.

ers (APCs) is out of date. If such forces encounter an enemy with like armament and firepower, they say, the war will degenerate into a stalemate because weapons have become so powerful and accurate that neither side will be able to move for fear of being destroyed. That is to say, the weapons will essentially cancel each other out. To avoid this, the theoreticians call for much lighter, more maneuverable forces, largely deployed by helicopters, that can work with heavier weapons to achieve a decision.

The analysts' urging to reorganize American military forces to reduce reliance on heavy, relatively slow, and relatively easy-to-hit weapons will lead to a more flexible and mobile army that can respond to any threat.

Let us examine the current status of American ground forces, how they have been organized to fight a comparably armed enemy (the Soviet Union), and what theoreticians believe must be done to give American forces decisive advantages against any enemy they're likely to face. The tactics now being developed can be adapted to whatever wars we fight, whether conventional against heavily armed enemies or low-intensity against light forces.

For most of World War II onwards, the army achieved victory by having more firepower than its enemies. American material riches permitted U.S. armies to concentrate such massive quantities of artillery, automatic weapons, tanks, and ground-support bombers and fighters that they finally ground down the German and Japanese armies. It was similar firepower that permitted the United States, with far fewer troops than the Chinese Communists, to create a stalemate in the last two years of the Korean War.

Firepower has been the preferred choice because Americans abhor high casualties and would rather swap dollars for lives. As a result, the U.S. military has gained great public support by substituting shells, bombs, rockets, and bullets for high human losses in battle. In the Vietnam War this exchange reached its zenith. In this war we used twice the bombs and ammunition we expended in the whole of World War II. In one "search-and-destroy" mission in early 1966, for example, the 1st Cavalry Division fired off 132,000 artillery rounds to kill 1,342 Vietcong. That works out to a hundred artillery shells to destroy a single enemy soldier—not counting the many additional thousands of tons of bombs and other ordnance dropped on the enemy![2]

Emphasis on firepower led to a concentration on extremely "heavy" divisions—combat forces with large numbers of big cannons, main battle tanks, attack helicopters, APCs, and other weapons. Since our principal danger throughout the Cold War was from the Soviet Union, whose forces also were armed with massive weapons, the U.S. military became even more weapon heavy, and less mobile.

It may be difficult for civilians to understand, but the real purpose of heavy weapons is not to destroy enemy soldiers but to destroy enemy weapons. The rationale for this is, if our weapons can shatter the enemy's tanks, artillery, and other guns, then the enemy soldiers will be defenseless, and either be killed or wounded, or forced to surrender or flee.

Thus the principal job of a tank is to kill another tank. The principal job of artillery is counterbattery fire, to destroy the other side's guns and howitzers. This elementary fact has immense implications, and has governed warfare from the beginning. For thousands of years a battle has raged between

2. Krepinevich, 222.

the offense and the defense, between the missile that destroys and the armor that protects. In the days before firearms, for example, inventors developed three bows that could drive arrows through the armor of a mounted knight or horseman: the compound bow made of layered materials that increased its tensile strength, the crossbow, and the English longbow. These weapons, and the gunpowder-propelled balls from muskets and other firearms that followed, finally eliminated the armored knight.

Today the tension between offense and defense has created weapons of immense power on both sides, and this has resulted in a tactical impasse between like-armed powers.

On the missile or offensive side are rockets and other chemical-energy explosive devices that can be guided almost infallibly by radar or laser beams or infrared sensors to the most vulnerable top parts of armored vehicles, or that can be scattered as minefields in the paths of tanks. These devices can be delivered by attack airplanes or helicopters, by hand-held launching systems, or by artillery howitzers or rocket launchers.

On the armor or defensive side are similar chemical-energy devices that can search out and destroy attack helicopters, other aircraft, artillery, and rocket launchers. In addition, there are faster tanks, thicker metal armament, and composite and reactive armors that absorb much of the energy of explosive devices before they can penetrate.[3]

This standoff has produced arguments about which weapons armies should emphasize, and thus how battles should be fought.

3. Reactive armor consists of boxlike slabs attached to a tank's existing armor. A strike against these slabs triggers a reactive explosive that prevents penetration.

Armor advocates maintain that defensive measures are more than a match for offensive chemical-energy antitank missiles. Besides, they say, tanks are only one-seventh as expensive as attack helicopters (like the Apache which performed well in the Persian Gulf War and is being upgraded with a new and more versatile radar-guided Hellfire missile). Thus tanks provide more bang for the buck than attack helicopters.

Furthermore, armor advocates say, the real tank killer that is likely to dominate in the next quarter-century is the kinetic-energy (or solid projectile) weapon. This weapon will probably use liquid or electro-magnetic propulsion, generating immense muzzle velocities that will penetrate any tank's armor.[4] In effect, the kinetic-energy weapon is a high-tech modern version of the antitank gun of World War II. The most famous of these was the German 88-millimeter gun, designed as an antiaircraft weapon, but possessing such high muzzle velocity that Erwin Rommel and other German commanders found it was incomparable in penetrating Allied armor.

The kinetic-energy weapon will be far too heavy to be carried by a helicopter. It will be mounted on a tank chassis, and will, in effect, be a tank. Armor advocates, therefore, see the kinetic-energy missile as the principal armored weapon, and the role of tanks will remain to kill other tanks.[5]

All of these arguments are cited by the offensive school as precisely why armor cannot be the "master weapon" of

4. The American kinetic-energy system under development is the line-of-sight antitank (LOSAT) weapon, to be mounted on a Bradley fighting vehicle chassis and capable of defeating all predicted future armored vehicles. See *Army* magazine, October 1993, 314.

5. Swinburn, 35–37.

the future. Army Major Anthony M. Coroalles argues that, on balance, the deck is stacked against armor.[6] Highly accurate chemical-energy missiles will destroy many tanks, despite their defenses, he says. The danger of hits will slow the movement of tanks, while electronic sensors and other devices that alert the enemy to the presence of armor will force tanks to disperse. This will make their control more difficult. Finally, the armor defenses that do foil missile attacks also contribute to making armor less mobile. Higher speed and mounting heavy reactive armor means greater fuel use, and this puts additional strain on logistics, or getting fuel up to the tanks.[7]

We now must examine how battles are actually won. Unless one side is overwhelmingly superior and bowls over the weaker force, the essential formula of victorious battle is a convergent assault. A commander achieves this by dividing the attacking force into two or more segments. The ideal method is for each segment to attack the same target at the same time but from a different direction or approach. This holds the entire enemy force in the grip of battle and prevents any one portion from aiding the others. Sometimes a part of the force "fixes" the enemy in place or distracts him while the other part maneuvers to gain surprise and break up the defense.

6. Coroalles, 62–72.

7. Analysts listed high fuel use as a shortcoming of the Abrams M1A1 tank during the Gulf War. See *Conduct of the Persian Gulf War*, 751. The XM8 armored gun system (AGS), which will replace the M551A1 Sheridan light tank, deals with the problem of weight by tailoring armor packages to meet expected threats. The base or lowest version with the least armor weighs just under 20 tons, the highest, 25.5 tons. The base AGS gets approximately two miles to a gallon of fuel at cruising speed. See *Army* magazine, June 1994, 69.

World War II American General George S. Patton crystallized the concept most colorfully when he said his troops could defeat the enemy by "holding him by the nose, as you kick him in the ass."

The classic example of the convergent assault was Alexander the Great's battle against the Indian King Porus on the Hydaspes (Jhelum) River in the Punjab in 326 B.C. By a series of feints and threats, Alexander misled Porus into believing he was going to cross the river near present-day Haranpur, thereby drawing the entire Indian army there. Leaving part of the Macedonian army at Haranpur, Alexander led a strong selected force some fourteen miles upstream one night, and crossed to the opposite (eastern) bank. Alexander annihilated a small Indian force sent to stop him, then marched on Porus's flank and rear. When Porus turned to meet Alexander, the Macedonians at Haranpur crossed the river and descended on Porus's rear. The result was the destruction of Porus's entire army.[8]

Another example was in 1632 during the Thirty Years War when Sweden's Gustavus Adolphus set up guns and burned straw to create a smoke screen while forcing one point on the Lech River in Bavaria. This held Marshal Tilly of Austria in place while another Swedish force crossed the Lech on a bridge of boats a mile upstream. Assailed from two directions simultaneously, Tilly was unable to defend either point and was defeated, Tilly himself being killed.

Current army doctrine is to fight battles similar to what Alexander and Gustavus Adolphus conducted, using fixing

8. For an analysis of Alexander's battle along the Hydaspes, see J. F. C. Fuller, *The Generalship of Alexander the Great* (New Brunswick, N. J.: Rutgers University Press, 1960; reprint New York: Da Capo, 1989), 180–99.

forces and one or more maneuver forces. However, the army at present sees the maneuver force as consisting largely of men in tanks, self-propelled artillery, or APCs.

But such a force, says Major Coroalles, no longer will succeed against a first-rate opponent—because the missiles the opponent fires will slow or disperse armor and APCs to such a degree that a fast decision will be impossible. "It is probable," says Coroalles, "that in a future war, ground armored movement will be stopped as cold as infantry movement was during World War I," when artillery, machine guns, barbed wire, and fortifications solidified battle into immobile trench warfare. If armor remains the main maneuver force, war will turn into a stalemate and static warfare, as happened in World War I.

Coroalles and other army thinkers say the only solution is to restore mobility by the use of helicopters—that is, air-assault infantry and light artillery as the maneuver force. Throughout history, the faster armies generally have won, because their elements could reach decisive points before the enemy or, by concentrating an overwhelming force, evict smaller enemy forces from such points.

Using choppers to carry and protect them, air-delivered maneuver troops can move at ten times the speed of any land weapon. Helicopter refueling and maintenance can be provided well to the rear, thus choppers are logistically less vulnerable than armor, which must have these elements brought up to them. Finally, helicopters can fly over the enemy and overwhelm an army operating at the pace of armor.

Other exponents of helicopter-borne maneuver forces include Colonel Richard Sinnreich, former director of the School of Advanced Military Studies at Fort Leavenworth,

Kansas, and Colonel Harry E. Rothmann of the National War College, Washington.[9] Sinnreich compares forces maneuvered by air to armored forces that moved on the ground in World War II. Rothmann agrees with Coroalles that air-maneuver forces can become the decisive striking element, preparing the way for ground-maneuver elements to complete the victory.[10]

This would be analogous, for example, to how Heinz Guderian's fast German panzer divisions broke into the rear of British and French armies in France in 1940. The Allies were operating at the "methodical battle" pace of their artillery and infantry formations, implying a timed movement of men and material to generate maximum firepower under central control.[11] The radical difference in speed or pace between the panzers and the Allied forces permitted the German tanks to mass against a single enemy point before the French could reinforce it, break through, and open the way for following German foot and mechanized divisions to destroy the outflanked Allies.

The current military view is that chopper-borne units complement ground forces—that is, they help the dominant land forces to win the battle, but themselves are not the decisive element. The new school sees the matter precisely

9. Rothmann. See also "The Air Assault Division and Brigade Operations Manual," 101st Airborne Division (Air Assault), Fort Campbell; Kentucky, August 1, 1988.

10. Some analysts see future warfare being based on a "battle of convergence," that is, concentrating overwhelming force at a decisive point at high speed. Forces would move dispersed into jumpoff positions, and only concentrate on the field of battle, both by air and on the ground. See Major James M. Toguchi and James Hogue, "The Battle of Convergence in Four Dimensions," *Military Review*, 72; 10 (October 1992), 11–20.

11. Coroalles, 66.

reversed: ground forces help the aerial forces, which do have the decisive job.

The American military leadership came to its present orthodoxy after the Vietnam War. In Vietnam, American forces recognized the value of combining helicopter-delivered forces and helicopter attacks with land-based forces and practiced it widely, though seldom in the coordinated fashion envisioned by today's advocates. But, says Rothmann, in the years after Vietnam U.S. leaders focused on a heavy weapons battle in Europe with the Soviet Union and lost sight of the air-maneuver combined-arms concept.

This deemphasis of helicopter-borne attacks grew as sophisticated air defenses developed and leaders feared that helicopters had become too vulnerable. Opponents pointed to high chopper losses in the South Vietnamese invasion of Laos in February and March, 1971, which tried, but failed, to disrupt the enemy supply line (Ho Chi Minh Trail) from North to South Vietnam. In this operation, the United States lost 90 of 659 helicopters used to airlift South Vietnamese soldiers, while 453 were damaged.[12]

Yet Rothmann points out that the loss rate per 1,000 hours of flying in the operation was only 1.01 choppers. Also, helicopters were invaluable to Britain in the Falklands War of 1982 and to the Soviets in their invasion of Afghanistan in the 1980s, despite losses from Stinger missiles supplied by the United States to Afghan rebels. In the Israeli incursion into Lebanon in 1982–85, Israeli forces found that helicopters were survivable and effective. In all of these conflicts, helicopters permitted maneuver on the battlefield.

Coroalles, Sinnreich, and Rothmann see aerial combined

12. Young, 253.

arms as the striking force, while heavy ground forces (including armor)[13] serve as the fixing or holding force. Helicopters can't close with the enemy and hold terrain. However, they can deliver well-armed infantry, light artillery, and other weapons to a decisive point, and these can close with the enemy and join with the heavier-weaponed holding force to reach a victory on the ground.

Advocates thus see chopper-borne maneuver forces and heavy or armored forces as being two parts of a single tactical team that jointly wins a battle. This implies that forces will be delivered by helicopter to those points on the flank or rear that assist in distracting or diverting the enemy force. The distances implied in air-delivery are not necessarily great and are determined, not by the capability of choppers to fly long distances, but by the demands of the tactical mission. Thus a heliborne force might move only a few miles—or a score—but only to achieve, with the tank-led heavy holding force, the defeat of a particular enemy element.

Soviet leaders came to use similar methods in the later stages of the war in Afghanistan. They found that most Soviet commanders and troops were incurably "road bound"—that is, they were reluctant to leave the relative safety of their armored vehicles and pursue on foot Afghan rebels hiding in the mountains. This essentially left the countryside in the hands of the enemy. To counteract the tendency, Soviet leaders increasingly relied on heliborne and parachute troops to seize particular Afghan objectives. Soviet leaders also found

13. In actual combat, armor doesn't usually operate alone. It most often is accompanied by mechanized infantry and self-propelled artillery, which together form a single team. The army refers to such combinations as "heavy" forces. Consequently, references to "armor" or "tanks" in this book normally imply operations with infantry, tanks, and artillery.

that tanks in Afghanistan served as little more than fire platforms against enemy fire platforms. That is, tanks ceased to be major maneuver elements that brought about a decisive victory. Instead, they became merely guns.[14]

Both Russian and American forces are moving toward heliborne forces as maneuver elements. This begs the question as to whether this won't create the same potential stalemate as exists today between two sophisticated forces. The answer is yes, with one caveat: air-delivered forces will restore movement to the battlefield, and this will open opportunities for resourceful commanders. Weapons, tactics, and doctrine have usually been comparable on both sides throughout history. One side achieved victory by bringing forth a leader, like Napoleon Bonaparte, Stonewall Jackson, William Tecumseh Sherman, or Erwin Rommel, who, with the tools and techniques of war he was handed, won victories by surprise, deception, speed, and resolve.

Since new doctrine will require division-sized forces designed around the helicopter, the present-day heavy division—built to fight similarly heavy Soviet divisions, and still the mainstay of the army combat force—is an anachronism.

Colonel Rothmann has proposed a radically new structure that accommodates air-maneuverability. He and other army leaders also are calling for the great bulk of the U.S. Army and Marine Corps to be stationed inside the continental United States. A half-century of large garrisons in foreign lands will come to an end. There are still advocates of a strong U.S. military presence in Europe and in Korea, primarily for political reasons to buttress NATO in one case, and the

14. Stephen Blank, "Afghanistan and Beyond: Reflections on the Future of Warfare," 226–27.

threat of another invasion of South Korea by North Korea in the other.

Though the United States will probably keep some forces in both places, the principal permanent American presence in potential danger spots is more likely to consist of forward-deployed logistical and intelligence units, plus headquarters, or small, elite leadership groups, which can calculate responses to dangers that occur and take charge of ground reinforcements as they arrive.

The most logical source of these reinforcements would be joint task forces (JTF), one near each coast of the United States, and capable of rapid movement by air and sea to any place on earth where the United States decides to exert its power. Colonel Rothmann has proposed such a structure, and army tendencies are leaning in this or similar directions.[15] In 1993 Lieutenant General John H. Tilelli, Jr., deputy army chief of staff for operations, said that "doctrine recognizes that the army of the twenty-first century will be a force-projection army, that it must be capable of rapid deployment from the continental United States and ready to fight upon entry into an overseas theater of operations."[16]

Joint task forces would mean a radically different army from the force based around heavy weapons and main battle tanks that stood in the path of a possible Soviet invasion of Western Europe for two generations. Rothmann recommends that each joint task force be built around an army corps of four divisions—two air-assault divisions (helicop-

15. *United States Army Posture Statement for the Financial Year 1994*, 62–63, projects two army divisions in Germany and one in South Korea by 1995, with eight active contingency and reinforcement divisions, plus eight reserve and two cadre (leadership-only) divisions, in the United States.

16. Lieutenant General John H. Tilelli, Jr. *Army* magazine, October 1993, 144.

ter-borne), one light armored division (equipped with light-armored vehicles and the projected armored gun system [AGS] or light tank), and one heavy division. In addition, the JTF postulated by Rothmann would include a U.S. Marine Corps expeditionary force, an air force tactical wing, and air and sea lift that could move the task force, or elements of it.

Rothmann also proposes building a heavy corps of two divisions, plus reserve components, within the continental United States. Their use would be primarily for sustained land battle in Europe and a hedge against a more bellicose policy of Russia. But elements of this corps could reinforce the lighter corps wherever heavy forces are needed. The heavy corps would be built around formidable artillery and missile weapons, and the army's main battle tank, the improved Abrams M1A2 with heavy armor and a powerful 120-millimeter gun.

A joint task force on the west coast could move within hours or days toward any challenge across the Pacific, while one on the east coast could respond to a crisis in Europe, the Middle East or Africa. Forces from either task force could move south into Latin America, if needed.

Although the U.S. Army at present is emphasizing its awesome firepower, the new methods implied by air-assault forces will insure that maneuver will characterize future wars.[17]

---

17. Sullivan and Dubik, 20–21: "When land forces began to include machine-powered air systems—the utility, cargo, scout, and attack helicopters—the conditions were set for another leap in land maneuver. . . . At each step, improved maneuver capability contributed to the land combat commander's ability to move over increasingly dispersed areas and converge quickly at the decisive point, thus concentrating effects of both fires and maneuver."

This is not only because of the impasse that has developed between offensive and defensive weapons but because weapons and sensors are becoming so accurate and sensitive that toe-to-toe slugfests of weapon against weapon, such as was envisioned in a confrontation with the Soviet Union, are no longer reasonable. No other country has the military hardware to challenge American weapons. Other countries will conduct their wars to avoid U.S. firepower, not stand up against it.

Air-maneuver divisions may offer a means of restoring mobility to operations, and may offer a way to come to grips with the extreme accuracy and lethality of modern weapons. These two factors have altered the nature of battle fundamentally and have made conflict so dangerous that battlefields no longer will resemble those of previous wars.[18]

18. The following are the major offensive weapons either operational or under development in the U. S. Army: (1) Armored gun system (AGS), a direct-fire 105-millimeter cannon that will replace the M551 Sheridan light tank; air-transportable; armor protection against hand-held anti-tank weapons; range 460 kilometers (km), top speed 45 miles per hour. (2) Javelin antitank missile, 49 pounds, portable by one man, lethal against all tanks, range 2,000 meters; a fire-and-forget weapon that permits the gunner to lock on the target and immediately take cover; the missile attacks the top (weakest) part of the enemy tank. (3) OH-58D Kiowa Warrior armed scout helicopter (to be replaced by the RAH-66 Comanche early in the next century); navigation system permits precision target-location at standoff ranges; fires Stinger air-to-air and Hellfire and Hydra air-to-ground missiles. (4) TOW improved target-acquisition system, a highly mobile, all-weather, day and night long-range weapon capable of destroying all armor. (5) RAH-66 Comanche, the army's next-generation armed reconnaissance helicopter; operable in all terrain, adverse weather, day or night; range 1,260 km; weapons air-to-air and air-to-ground missiles, turret-mounted 20mm cannon; able to direct fire on targets from other weapons. (6) Advanced field artillery system (AFAS), will provide mobile, lethal, more survivable, self-propelled artillery, using liquid propellant. (7) Paladin M109A6 155mm self-propelled howitzer, the primary indirect fire support weapon; within 60 seconds Paladin can receive a fire mission

Although armor advocates hold that tanks are still doing a good job of fending off chemical-energy explosives in missiles, the offensive missile appears to be winning its contest with defensive armor. Missiles now have enormous power

while on the move, stop and deliver an accurate first-round shell day or night; rocket-assisted projectile range 30 km, unassisted 24 km. (8) Army tactical missile system (ATACMS) can hit land targets at ranges beyond those of cannons, rockets and Lance missiles; a semiguided ballistic missile fired from the multiple-launch rocket system (MLRS). (9) Tri-service standoff attack missile (TSSAM), a tactical cruise missile that can strike moving armor and other high-priority targets out to 100 nautical miles and beyond; launched from the MLRS; carries 22 brilliant anti-armor submunitions (BAT). (10) Brilliant antiarmor submunitions (BAT), a three-foot glider with acoustic and infrared sensors that can autonomously locate moving tanks and other armor; its shaped-charge warhead can defeat any armor; 22 to be carried in the TSSAM missile and six in the ATACMS. (11) Multiple-launch rocket system (MLRS), a free-flight artillery rocket system with current ranges beyond 30 km, to be extended to beyond 45 km; twelve-round launcher on mobile tracked vehicle with "shoot-and-scoot" tactics to reduce danger of counterbattery fire; basic rocket 13 feet long; a sense-and-destroy armor (SADARM) program projects submunitions which, after ejection from the MLRS rocket or 155mm howitzer projectile, will search for armor and, if found, will fire an armor-piercing projectile at it. (12) Special operations aircraft (SOA), modified MH-60K Black Hawk and MH-47E Chinook helicopters using infrared sensors and radar that permit forces to fly at low altitudes, at night, in bad weather and at long ranges while following but avoiding terrain below. (13) M1A2 Abrams main battle tank with 120-mm gun and heavy armor protection. (14) Bradley fighting vehicle (BFV), lightly armored, full-tracked, providing mobility, some firepower (25mm chain gun, machine gun and TOW antitank missiles) and protection against small-arms and artillery fire for infantry and cavalry. (15) Longbow Apache, a program to use all laser Hellfire missiles and the new Hellfire radar frequency (RF) fire-and-forget anti-armor missile on the remanufactured AH-64D Apache attack helicopter; a radar antenna detects targets that the Apache can attack itself or pass on to other aircraft or ground weapons; pilots can engage up to 16 targets in less than a minute. (16) Line-of-sight antitank (LOSAT) weapon, firing a kinetic-energy missile that will defeat all armor. (17) Non-line-of-sight combined arms (NLOS-CA), a weapon that will destroy armor and other targets well beyond the maximum range of tank guns or direct-fire antitank missiles. See *Army* magazine, October, 1993, 240–314; October, 1994, 233–319; *Conduct of the Persian Gulf War*, 738–88.

and almost inconceivable accuracy. They cannot always destroy armor or fortifications, but they frequently can.

By means of the "Navstar" global-positioning system (GPS), American bombs, missiles, rockets, and shells can be guided to within thirty-eight feet of any point on earth. Navstar is based on signals from twenty-four earth-orbiting satellites. During the Gulf War, bombers, fighters and helicopters were able to direct their bombs and missiles to the exact locations of Iraqi targets by means of GPS. The navy guided its Tomahawk cruise missile through doors and other openings to demolish highly fortified Iraqi targets. By comparison, Iraq's Scud missiles used primitive guidance systems, based on coordinates from inaccurate maps, and often missed their targets by several miles.

Today almost all countries can develop weapons using GPS technology. They can exploit the system through a program the Federal Aviation Administration has made available to airlines, so commercial aircraft can make precision landings in bad weather. GPS satellites send two navigation signals. The one available to airlines has a built-in error, but permits coming within 328 feet of any location on the planet. The second signal, which broadcasts the correct information, can be received only by U. S. military equipment. However, other countries, employing the FAA commercial system, can break the military code by use of computers and ground-based radio beacons. This means that potential enemies can develop a "poor man's cruise missile" and other weapons-targeting systems that are as accurate as American types.[19]

GPS, coupled with laser, radar, and infrared weapons-guidance systems, now virtually can guarantee first-strike ac-

19. John J. Fialka, "Airliners Can Exploit U.S. Guidance System, But So Can Enemies," *Wall Street Journal*, August 26, 1993, A1.

curacy. There is countertechnology which permits a defender to home in on an incoming round by means of radar and other sounding devices, and, by fast computer backtracking of the round's trajectory, pinpoint the location of the firing gun, tank, or missile launcher, and calculate an immediate counterstrike. This makes counterfire extremely deadly. The danger has generated the development of "fire-and-forget" weapons that permit the launcher to lock on to a target, fire, then move fast to avoid a counterstrike. His missile meanwhile goes straight to the target.

First-strike accuracy and fire-and-forget weapons mean that no place on the battlefield is safe. Virtually any target that can be located and is within the range of an offensive weapon can be hit, along with the soldiers manning it.

Aside from armor, there are two fundamental methods that American forces can employ to reduce the effect of missile accuracy and counterstrikes: dispersion and denying the enemy the latest technology. Both are, at best, limited responses.

All armies now require their troops to spread out, relying on improved communications to permit commanders to control them wherever they're located. In World War II, 100,000 men usually occupied no more than 2,750 square kilometers of territory, whereas in the Persian Gulf War of 1991, the same number of troops occupied almost a hundred times as much geographical space.[20]

Lack of cover encouraged such extreme dispersion in the deserts of Iraq, Kuwait, and Saudi Arabia. But the days of massed armies have passed forever. Now, even platoon-sized concentrations (fifty men or so) are rare, and the picture of

20. Sullivan and Dubik, 13.

"shoot-and-scoot" weapons firing, then immediately "displacing" or moving has become so routine that it is the stuff of Madison Avenue advertising. Here's an example by General Electric's Textron Lycoming division from *Army* magazine:

You're in the belly of an armored vehicle known as AFAS, advanced field artillery system. And things are happening very fast. You've just delivered fire-for-effect at an unseen enemy over 40 klicks [kilometers] away. Before they reach the top of their trajectory, your shells are acquired by their radar. Immediately, an enemy fire-control officer punches a computer, locking in your location. Within seconds, the counter battery is in the air. Guided by lasers. Incredibly accurate. Coming right down your muzzle. But you're not there. Throttle open, you execute a survivability move in record time. Then you set up and fire again. And move again. Set up and fire. Move. You've got it knocked. You've got it down. You've got an LV100 gas turbine engine [made by Lycoming].[21]

Superior technology at the moment insures that American weapons are able to hit an enemy when, in most cases, the enemy cannot hit U.S. forces. The United States, for example, is developing JSTARS (joint surveillance target attack radar system) that can detect moving and fixed targets so accurately that American weapons can strike with precision at extended ranges. JSTARS is based on air force E-8 aircraft, militarized Boeing 707 airliners, that can orbit within friendly territory but cover a wide and deep enemy region with radar.[22]

American defensive weapons—that is, devices that de-

21. *Army,* October 1993, 8–9.

22. JSTARS is a joint army-air force program. The air force also has the similar four-engine E-3 Awacs (airborne warning and control system), which provides the same sort of airborne surveillance and command functions for tactical and air defense forces. It detects enemy aircraft, controls

stroy incoming enemy missiles—also remain superior. The Patriot, which, despite failures, knocked down a number of Iraqi Scud missiles in the Gulf War, is being upgraded to enhance its accuracy against shorter-range ballistic missiles and air-breathing threats, such as cruise missiles or advanced manned aircraft. The United States also is developing THAAD (theater high-altitude area defense) which will fire hypervelocity missiles that will collide with and destroy enemy missiles at high altitudes, minimizing debris and other damage. The army is producing the Avenger air-defense system, firing improved Stinger missiles, which will provide air defense for units as small as regiments.

JSTARS and other locating devices have led army leaders to state that American forces will be capable in the twenty-first century of detecting the enemy at extended, over-the-horizon distances while remaining invisible to the enemy.[23]

However, the United States is selling a great deal of its sophisticated weapons to foreign countries. This, and the fact that the global-positioning system has been distributed by the Federal Aviation Administration, demonstrates that the United States may not be able to maintain its technological lead indefinitely.[24]

---

defensive tactical fighters and strike aircraft, and provides a long-range air picture for commanders. The navy has the two-engine E-2C Hawkeye, a carrier-capable aircraft which can range ahead of carrier task forces and provide early warning of attacks or dangers. See *Conduct of the Persian Gulf War*, 681–85, 709–11.

23. Sullivan and Dubik, 24. This means that the military will have the capability of finding the enemy or hiding from the enemy, but the fog of war and friction in every battlefield situation will prevent the application of this capability in every instance.

24. Jeff Cole and Sarah Lurman, "Weapons Merchants Are Going Great Guns in Post-Cold War Era," *Wall Street Journal*, January 28, 1994, A1.

In summary, the United States ground forces in the future will project their power primarily from North America, using air and sea lift capability and relying on the U.S. Navy and Air Force to maintain free seas and open skies to whatever location we decide to strike. American land forces will emphasize light, highly maneuverable units, largely based on helicopters and fast, mostly armored vehicles, including self-propelled artillery and missile-launchers. The walking infantry of past wars will be no more, but soldiers may dismount when they reach their objectives and still occupy the ground on foot.

Ground forces will place less dependence on heavy weapons, like main battle tanks and artillery that are not immediately "displacable." This is because the enemy will not concentrate his forces to allow Americans to destroy them easily. We also will deemphasize heavy tanks and immobile weapons because they can be destroyed in short order if the enemy can locate them.

Ground forces will operate in much smaller units than in past wars, but each group will command far more powerful and varied weapons than previously. These small forces will constitute battle groups. That is, they will consist of mixed arms, of what we today look upon as infantry, artillery, helicopter, and armored weapons. In World War II, Korea, and Vietnam, we routinely mixed arms within divisions and in some cases down to regiments. In the future, these battle groups or combined-arms teams will go down to company level, that is, around 150 to 200 men. They will operate helicopters, trucks, light tanks, armored personnel carriers, armored infantry fighting vehicles, self-propelled artillery, and protected support vehicles. In many cases, these weapons will be delivered to the battlefield by helicopters.[25]

Consequently, mobility will be great, firepower per man will be high, and accuracy of weapons guided by radar, laser, and other sounding devices near perfect.

But the flip side is that, except for our helicopters, we will depend upon roads to move in most places, and everywhere we will require a long and heavy supply train to our rear to bring up fuel, ammunition, and food. In other words, the ground forces will still be locked to the same high technology and intricate logistics chain that the Chinese in Korea and the Communists in Vietnam exploited to our detriment. Our enemies will likewise wield more firepower per man and our accurate shots can be answered almost instantaneously by equally accurate counterfire.

Finally, the kinds of wars we will face will be conditioned by the very superiority the United States possesses. Although the United States must be prepared to meet any threat, it is unlikely to be defied by a power equal to it in military strength and technology. But this does not mean that we necessarily will succeed. Challengers will rarely risk slugging it out head to head with American forces in conventional battle because of fear they will suffer Iraq's fate in the Gulf War. Challengers most likely will try to draw American forces into invading their territories, where they can counter U.S. weapons's supremacy by indirect means.

We must now examine why powers that engage in aggressive war by invading another country do not automatically win wars when they have greater military strength. In the chapters ahead I will examine how weaker powers in the twentieth century achieved their aims by striking at more

25. Sullivan and Dubik, 20.

powerful opponents' vulnerabilities while avoiding their strengths. I will also show how these weaker powers have operated in disparate climates, conditions, and technologies, and how the principles they employed are applicable today.

I will study the Boers of South Africa who stopped Britain, the greatest imperial power on earth at the start of the century; the Bedouins of Arabia, who, led by T. E. Lawrence, helped to defeat Turkey in World War I and gained their claim to independence; the Chinese Communists who defeated the much-stronger Nationalist Chinese, undermined the Japanese occupation of north China, and whose leader Mao Zedong crystallized doctrines of irregular warfare with great clarity; and the Vietnamese Communists who defeated France and the United States in a struggle extending over a generation.

At the conclusion, I will summarize the lessons these wars have taught us and what they portend for wars in the future.

FIVE

The Boer War: Prologue to the Future

T HE BOER OR SOUTH AFRICAN WAR, 1899–1902, between Britain and two small white republics, was the first conflict since the Spanish guerrilla war against Napoleon that demonstrated the capability of a militarily feeble but resolute people to defy a world power.

Britain fought the Boer War against two small republics, the Orange Free State and Transvaal. But the war represented a clash between two disparate ways of life: between Britain, a world power then at the height of its imperial and industrial might, and the Boers, a rural, conservative, deeply religious Calvinist people of mainly Dutch, French Huguenot, and German stock who had occupied the land after the first Dutch settlers landed at the Cape of Good Hope in 1652. The lessons taught in that war had to be relearned time after time during the next nine decades by every power that tried to overwhelm a weak but similarly determined people elsewhere in the world. They are still valid today.

Only Britain itself successfully applied the principle that was demonstrated in the Boer War. In the 1950s it promised the people of Malaya political freedom and, by giving the Malayans what they most desired, undermined a Communist insurgency there.[1]

Although Britain finally won the South African War in theory, it actually granted the Boers what they had been fighting for: ultimate independence; guarantee that their Dutch-dialect language, Afrikaans, an essential element of their cultural identity, would be retained, and agreement not to allow the overwhelmingly more numerous blacks in South Africa to gain political rights. For most of the twentieth century the Boers or Afrikaners, now largely allied with British settlers, maintained white dominance. Only in 1994, after decades of violence and strife (which followed conceptually the indirect tactics the Boers had used against the British), did the blacks at last gain control of South Africa.

The British would not have given the Boers what they wanted had it not been for their inability to crush the Afrikaners after they resorted to guerrilla warfare. This is true despite the fact that the British invented and employed excellent weapons—including the first "concentration camps" of displaced persons and families of Boer fighters, blockhouses to guard railways and protect supply lines, and a scorched-earth policy aimed at starving the Boers into submission. The blockhouses were useful but insufficient to stop the Boers. The camps and scorched earth were actually counter-productive to British aims. In the end, the British gained peace only by agreeing to fundamental Boer demands.

Many Boers had "trekked" or migrated into the Orange Free State and Transvaal after Britain emancipated their slaves in Cape Colony in 1833. They might have existed in-

1. For an analysis of the British strategy in Malaya, see Clutterbuck, 63–78.

definitely on their livestock and grain farms without British interference except for the discovery of enormous deposits of gold near Johannesburg in Transvaal in 1886. The Boers wanted to maintain their way of life, limit rights to "uitlanders" or foreign whites who flocked in, and preserve their domination of the blacks. But Britain wanted control of the gold. Thus a mighty confrontation became inevitable and it commenced in October, 1899.

The war started out as a conventional affair between two European peoples. But the Boers—who numbered fewer than 600,000, including those living under British rule in Cape Colony—lost quickly when they challenged British arms head to head. Only in June–September 1900, after they abandoned traditional warfare and broke their armies into small bodies of highly mobile horsemen, were they able to bewilder and defeat British regular forces. From then on, the guerrillas dictated the pace and the course of the action.

From the beginning, the Boers were unable to challenge the immensely superior firepower of the British army. Their one chance to win at least a campaign in a conventional war was to take advantage of the fact that Britain had few troops in South Africa and to race into Cape Colony and Natal, the other British colony in South Africa with a seacoast, and seize the major ports. This would have made it difficult for the British to land reinforcements.

However, the Boers as a people were uninterested in conquest, only in protecting their homeland from invasion. In addition, Boer military leadership was extremely unimaginative and hesitant. The two factors worked together to prevent swift drives to the ports. Instead, the Boer commanders made the worst of all decisions: they locked the bulk of their

forces into useless sieges of small British garrisons at Mafeking, the diamond-mining town of Kimberley, and Ladysmith. None of these towns was important strategically,
although Ladysmith, in Natal, was on the route to the port
of Durban. However, the Boers could have bypassed it and
pressed on to capture the port.

Since the Boers besieged these three towns, the British
were able to concentrate on relieving them, confident that
the Boers would be compelled to throw most of their
strength into efforts to stop them. Therefore, the Boers had
to fight a conventional war—that is, meet the British army
head to head. What was worse, they had to position themselves in front of the British at points the British could predict and plan for in advance, instead of embarking on other,
more dangerous adventures elsewhere.

Consequently, the Boers sacrificed their one great advantage: extreme mobility, made possible by the fact that nearly
every Boer was a horseman and knew his land intimately.
The Boers could ride around enemy forces, strike wherever
they chose, and swiftly disappear if a fight went against them.

From the beginning, the Boers could not match the overwhelming power of the British army. In any given fight the
British could bring to bear much superior firepower—which
in the period consisted principally of artillery. The British
possessed large numbers of field guns, the Boers only a few,
although these were French and German pieces of the latest
design. Inferiority in firepower was, of course, why the Boers
could not meet the British in conventional warfare. It is the
same reason today why other powers are unable to meet
American forces in a stand-up fight.

Due to the erroneous strategy of their leaders, however,
the Boers did attempt to do this. And for some weeks they

did not recognize that they were bound to fail. This was because of two factors: Boer possession of the German-made Mauser bolt-action rifle, and the abominable tactics practiced by the first British generals. Both factors worked together to delude the Boers into believing they could win, or at least stop the British, in a conventional war.

The Mauser rifle gave the Boers an early advantage. It could kill at 2,200 yards. This made it ideal for the high, open, largely treeless veldt or steppe where most of the war was fought. In this terrain the Boers, most of whom were marksmen, could mount effective rifle fire at long range. The Mauser could be fired twice as fast as British rifles because it was reloaded with the push of a thumb on a five-round clip while British cartridges had to be reloaded one at a time. The Mauser also did not inhibit Boer mobility on their native ponies.[2]

However, the Boer army was poorly organized for regular warfare. It was utterly unlike the British army, shaped in the traditional European and American pattern with rigid discipline, minute organization, and a deeply hierarchical structure directed by a professional officers corps.

The Boers possessed no officers corps. Their leaders were almost wholly amateurs and their armed forces consisted simply of all males aged sixteen to sixty, although males on both sides of the age frontiers actually served. When called

2. Neither the British nor the Boers caught on to the importance of the machine gun, a new weapon that was even more important because the recent development of smokeless powder made it difficult to locate when firing. Although Hiram Maxim had perfected the machine gun in 1884, both sides mounted .303-inch Maxims on carts and treated them more like artillery pieces than the portable automatic weapons they were—and became in World War I. Thus in South Africa the machine gun played no critical role. See Farwell, 43.

to duty, the Boers brought their own horses, bridles, saddles, rifles, and immediate rations. They enjoyed (or endured) neither formal military training, discipline, marching, saluting, pay, uniforms, nor insignia, and their ranks bore little resemblance to European standards. The Boers wore whatever civilian clothes they desired into battle, although the "uniform" soon came to be the usual, utilitarian Boer farmer's attire—broad-brimmed slouch hat, corduroy trousers, shirt, comfortable boots or shoes—plus a bandolier of rifle ammunition thrown over the shoulder.

Except for police units and artillery batteries, which possessed normal military structure, the Boer combat organization, the commando, was entirely geographical, not tactical, in concept. It consisted of every man in each of the forty electoral districts of the two republics. Thus, the commandos varied widely in size, from 300 to 3,000 men. Commando members elected a commandant. In larger commandos, they also elected field cornets for each electoral ward, and sometimes one or two assistant field cornets. In a few there was a further subdivision into sections under corporals. Each republic elected the head of its army, the commandant-general, and later there were assistant commandants-general and vecht ("fighting") generals.

Laws supposedly governed call to action, desertion, and leaves, but were seldom enforced. The Boer army was voluntary in the full sense of the term. When a Boer decided to leave, he left; when he wanted to return, he came back. A commandant could never be sure precisely how many men he had, but the system emphasized self-reliance and thinking for oneself. Indeed, Boers simply disregarded orders if they found them unacceptable. Commanders knew that the fainthearted quickly vanished and whoever was present was motivated and loyal. They also knew they could disband a party in a flash and reunite later at some assigned location, with virtually no danger of unit disintegration.

The commandos were awkward in conventional war, primarily because of their great variation in strength and the lack of a command hierarchy that could control and deploy commandos when several came together. Yet this weakness became a strength when the conventional war failed and the commando returned to its local base. There it could operate on its own, requiring little or no direction. Its independence encouraged members to exploit opportunities to attack small British detachments or posts, while it could mobilize, strike, and disappear or disperse within hours. Still, when the need arose, it could combine with nearby commandos for an extended campaign or for a concentrated blow against a larger British force.

There was one peculiarity about the Boers that dramatically limited their military capability: being a small minority in a huge land, they placed great value on human life and would not sacrifice a man for any purpose. Consequently, the Boers would retreat rapidly when a situation became dangerous, and, when cornered, would invariably surrender rather than fight to the last.[3]

Although sieges were the Boers' fatal strategic flaw, British leaders in the early stages of the war minimized the mistake because they insisted on advancing directly along the railways, in order for the troops to be guaranteed delivery of food, ammunition and other supplies. Because of this, the Boers at first climbed up on a mass of small hills (kops or

3. Belfield, 3–4, 28.

kopjes) dominating the railway and, looking out on superb fields of fire for their Mausers, dared the British to evict them.

The fundamental error of the original British commanding generals was to send their infantry directly against these kopjes. Battle after battle is a sorry tale of a British general rejecting any suggestion of a flanking or turning movement around an obstacle. Instead he would march his soldiers in plain view across the flat veldt or steppe. He would send them straight at the kopjes in formation—albeit in most cases extended or spread-out formation (five-pace intervals between men). To the marksmen Boers, the British soldiers offered perfect targets. Time after time Boer rifle fire would erupt from the kopjes, kill or wound numerous British soldiers, often halt the advance in its tracks, and sometimes leave the survivors pressed fearfully to the ground for hours at a time.

British junior officers and enlisted men finally realized their best bet was to rush somehow through the killing zone to the very base of the kopjes, where there was "dead ground," or an area that the Boers on the crests could not hit with their fire because of the bulge of the hills. In this safe zone the British could regroup and organize an assault up the kopjes. These, being usually rough and rocky, offered plenty of cover for the ascent. Whenever the British at last neared the top, the Boers almost invariably would retreat or surrender rather than close in hand-to-hand combat.

However, Transvaal General J. H. "Koos" De la Rey, 52 years old, soon recognized the mistake of Boers sitting on the hills and sent his men to dig trenches or foxholes in the flat veldt in front of the kopjes and then to camouflage the emplacements. From these holes the Boers could deliver "grazing fire" at ground level that was lethal two-thousand yards in front of them. De la Rey's idea was an independent discovery of a tactic that both sides in the American Civil War had exploited four decades before. The British had no counter for it, and, faced also with a high level of Boer marksmanship generally, their frontal attacks began to fail, threatening stalemate.

The new British commander, Field Marshal Lord Frederick Sleigh Roberts, who arrived in January 1900, and his chief of staff, Major General Lord Horatio Herbert Kitchener, saw the futility of direct assaults and broke the static war on the march to relieve Kimberley with a wide flanking movement to the east.

This quickly revealed how bankrupt was the strategy of the existing Boer leadership, for the commander opposing Roberts, Piet Cronje, refused to move from his "impregnable" position on the railway above the Modder River until it was too late. When he did move, he marched directly eastward toward where Lord Roberts was concentrating his army! The result was inevitable: Cronje's force was surrounded and, though a few resolute Boers broke out, Cronje surrendered 4,100 Boers east of Paardeberg in the Orange Free State on February 27, 1900.

General Sir Redvers Bullers, the British commander in Natal, failed miserably in a direct attack at Colenso on the Ţugela River along the railway leading to besieged Ladysmith. He finally attempted a flanking movement to the west. But it was so obvious and ponderous that the Boers occupied the heights on the north side of the Tugela before he could mount an attack. The major effort, when it came, was another direct assault, this time against the highest feature in the region, Spion Kop, 1,470 feet high. The peak had no significant tactical importance, since Bullers could have entirely avoided the hill mass that included Spion Kop by moving around it to the west. The battle resulted in a terrible defeat: 1,300 men lost, against about 300 Boers.

In February, 1900, Bullers reverted to another frontal assault in the Colenso area, which again had hard going until February 28, 1900, the day after Cronje's surrender near Paardeberg. This disaster so dejected the Boer defenders along the Tugela that they streamed back in confusion and disorder, abandoning the siege of Ladysmith, and climbing up on the heights of the Drakensberg Mountains, forming the Transvaal-Natal frontier.

It was now apparent to the Boers that they had no hope of defeating the British by conventional warfare. But they had not yet conceived of the possibilities of guerrilla war. Boer morale collapsed everywhere. Except for a fierce fight by De la Rey and South African Police at Driefontein, the Boers put up only sporadic resistance during the subsequent British march to the Orange Free State capital, Bloemfontein, seized by Roberts on March 13, 1900.

It was after this capture, which to the British seemed to signal the virtual end of the war, that Marthinus Theunis Steyn, president of the Free State, and some of the younger leaders prepared to wage guerrilla war. Their decision changed the nature of the conflict and preserved the Boer nation. In so doing, they showed the way for future weak countries to hobble the ambitions of stronger invaders.

SIX

Converting Stalemate to Victory

W**HEN A STRONGER POWER** invades a weaker country, it usually has one major advantage, superior military strength. However, it is hobbled by the hostility of the natives and their support of and assistance to domestic forces. This support nourishes the resolve of local forces to continue the struggle, while the reliable information natives can give about invaders' whereabouts often permits surprise attacks on detached invader units, bases, or transportation lines.

This was the situation that the British faced in South Africa. Their strength consisted of their much larger army with much greater firepower. Their weaknesses consisted of the antagonism of the Boer people, their inability to counter Boer mobility on the veldt, and the capability of Boers to strike against isolated British forces or important points. The British were in the same situation as the French in Spain during the Napoleonic wars: dependent upon extremely long and vulnerable lines of supply, and opposed by fiercely independent natives who knew the land intimately, had great flexibility, and, most of all, possessed the resolve to defeat the invader.

Yet strikes at isolated targets in themselves will not bring a decision, or force withdrawal of the enemy. There is rarely hope of winning a military victory over a superior enemy invader. Even so, a military stalemate is possible. However, this stalemate is likely to be most effective in influencing, not the invading army itself, but the people at home who support that army. Their potential war-weariness is the Achilles' heel of the invader. When the invaded country recognizes this fundamental weakness of the invader, it has the keys to victory.

The final stage of the Boer War represents how a military stalemate can achieve peace on terms favorable to the weaker country. The British people were stunned and incredulous as the war continued for two years after it had been theoretically ended with the captures of the Boer capitals of Bloemfontein and Pretoria. They were depressed with mounting totals of killed and wounded, with no end in sight. They were exasperated at the cost of maintaining an army in excess of 250,000 men that could not eliminate 15,000 Boers fighting them. Finally, they were scandalized and embarrassed by revelations that the British army had methodically destroyed most farmsteads of the Afrikaner people, leaving the women and children destitute, then had herded 120,000 Afrikaners, mostly women and children, into filthy concentration camps with inadequate food, shelter, water, and sanitary facilities, where more than 20,000 people died, the majority children.

Primarily because of the farm burnings and concentration camps, the Boer War became a moral issue in Britain and throughout the world. The British government which directed the conflict and the British army which carried it out became objects of revulsion in many countries. Now being labeled as child killers and oppressors, British government leaders sought for a way out that would gain as much as possible of their war aims and salvage something of their shattered reputations. Most of all, they sought a settlement that would prevent their being ousted at the next general election.

Revulsion by the public, both within one's own country and throughout the world, is the ultimate response to virtually all invaders who are unable to conclude a war in a timely fashion. As the war goes on and costs and losses mount, exasperation on the part of the invader's military forces inevitably will produce morally repugnant actions that will brand that power as arrogant, oppressive, and inhuman. In South Africa, the British burned farms and corraled women and children and were branded as murderers. Sixty-five years later in South Vietnam, Americans were likewise branded as murderers because soldiers sometimes killed civilians in their efforts to find and destroy Vietcong soldiers.

When moral outrage is joined in the public mind with excessive costs in lives and money, the people will become so agitated that the government will be forced to agree to peace. This occurred in Britain in 1902 in regard to South Africa, in France in 1954 and in the United States in 1973 in regard to Vietnam, and in the Soviet Union in 1989 in regard to its occupation of Afghanistan.

The government of the aggressor country, when it faces exploding opposition, will no longer demand total victory, and will seek the appearance of success rather than the reality of success. This is why a stalemate nearly always will give the weaker country the essentials of what it is seeking. Thus a guerrilla force that merely maintains itself against a major power will succeed, over time.

The Boers did not see the possibility of victory when they decided to abandon conventional war and move to guerrilla operations. They based their decision on their hostility to the British, who were seeking to take away their cherished independence. They knew it was hopeless to confront the British army directly. They saw guerrilla warfare as the only way to continue the fight.

Unlike the Vietnamese forty-five years later, the Boers possessed no philosopher like Ho Chi Minh who was able to convince many Vietnamese that their fight for independence was a war between the forces of good (the nationalists, as directed by the Communists) and the forces of evil (the imperialists, as represented by France).

The Boers thus were unable to elevate their cause into some Mithraic–Manichaean struggle between light and darkness. Rather it was based on desperation and the fact that one particular Boer leader discovered a way to succeed against overwhelming British power. This commander was Christiaan De Wet, forty-six years old. On March 31, 1900, De Wet led 1,600 men to destroy the Bloemfontein waterworks near Sannah's Post, about twenty-five miles east of the capital. While there he discovered a British detachment marching on Bloemfontein. De Wet ambushed the force, killing or wounding 170 men and capturing more than 400.

On April 4 near Dewetsdorp, De Wet struck against another isolated British garrison. Again he achieved momentary superiority. After a stand of less than a day and the loss of 10 killed and 35 wounded, 546 regular British soldiers surrendered.

These unexpected victories showed the Boers a way to continue the war. As it went on, they realized they did not have to win, they needed only to exist, to stay alive and deny the British a victory. As the cost of the war and its futility were impressed on the British people, they would ultimately become disenchanted and lose faith in it. This became the Boer strategy. The British, by their farm burning and concentration camps, helped the Boers, because these actions guaranteed that the British would become pariahs in world opinion and make the war even more unpopular at home.

De Wet had little but his native intelligence and his experience on the veldt to go on, but he worked out a method that gave victory. He summarized his tactics as follows: "This war demanded rapidity of action more than anything else. We had to be quick at fighting, quick at reconnoitering, quick (if it became necessary) at flying!"[1] That is, the Boers had to find a British force, reconnoiter to determine that it was isolated, organize an attack on it, and then get away before a relieving force could be notified and come up. This is the essential formula of guerrilla tactical victory.

Using the same principles, guerrillas also can avoid destruction by a vastly superior enemy force on a "search-and-destroy" mission. Survival requires the same kinds of skills as battle: quick reaction, quick concentration, sometimes a quick blow at an isolated enemy detachment, and quick retreat or dispersal. Later guerrilla leaders in other places arrived at similar conclusions and realized that, by following these rules, they could prevent defeat—even if they could not produce military victory.

De Wet made two mistakes that proved his point. Near Wepener, on the border with Basutoland, he was incensed to find a 1,900-man garrison, mainly of Boers from Cape Colony who had joined the British ranks. He considered these men traitors to their people and wanted to storm the

---

1. Belfield, 96.

place. A direct assault against a prepared position is nearly always an error because it plays into the enemy's strength. De Wet's men refused to sustain the losses that would occur. De Wet then insisted on besieging the garrison for sixteen days. This also is nearly always wrong because it gives the enemy time to concentrate against the besiegers and sometimes surround and destroy them. Fortunately for De Wet, he learned of a relieving British force and got away in time.

From that point on De Wet strove never to try to improve on an advantage. Successes had to be quick and forces had to depart at speed. Mobility was everything. In most cases, this forced the Boers to abandon their prisoners of war, because they could not move at the pace of the commandos—and there was no Boer sanctuary where prisoners could be held in compounds. The usual solution was to strip the captured men of clothing and weapons and send them marching toward the nearest British detachment.[2]

Just as the guerrilla war was emerging from its gestation, the conventional war was coming to an end. On May 5, 1900, Lord Roberts launched what he believed was the final offensive: to capture Pretoria. The 15,000 Boers could do little against the 44,000 British and fell back northward. This opened a way for the British to send a flying column to relieve Mafeking, some two-hundred miles north of Kimberley. The column accomplished its task on May 16, 1900.

Roberts captured Johannesburg on May 30 and Pretoria on June 5.

Many of the Transvaal leaders were ready to sue for

2. The likelihood that they would be released safely and soon, although shorn of their dignity, doubtless induced many British soldiers to surrender when they otherwise might have fought to the end.

peace. But a new spirit, spurred on by spectacular successes of De Wet and other Free Staters, blossomed while Lord Roberts was marching on Pretoria. In three separate guerrilla strikes in a little more than a week, Free State Boers caused more than 1,500 casualties, whereas Roberts's entire drive on Pretoria cost the British 587 men.[3] These victories galvanized the Transvaalers and transformed their gloom into resolution to continue the war.

The Free Staters and Transvaalers were helped by the death, disappearance, or humiliation of their most unsuccessful leaders. Cronje had been captured. P. J. "Piet" Joubert, the slow-moving, indecisive commander in Natal, had died. And the unimaginative Transvaal President Paul Kruger left for Holland in September, giving up his presidency to Schalk Burger. In their places materialized a remarkably able group of younger leaders: De Wet, James Barry Hertzog and Pieter Henrick Kritzinger in the Free State, and Louis Botha, Koos de la Rey, and Ben Viljoen in Transvaal. Free State President M. T. Steyn had provided firm leadership from the start, and continued to exert it, while Cambridge-educated, 30-year-old Jan Smuts, who had been Kruger's state attorney, developed as a first-class guerrilla fighter.

The British policy of burning farm homes, outbuildings, and stored grain, destroying farm equipment, and killing livestock began slowly. While Lord Roberts was in command (to December 1900), he limited farm burning to those granges lying nearest a spot where Boers had cut a railway or telegraph line. But any burnings struck the Boers as heinous and designed to deprive the people of a means to live. Thus Boers who might have accepted British victory, became ir-

3. Belfield, 102.

reconcilable enemies and were prepared to do anything to stop them.

In July 1900, British Lieutenant General Sir Archibald Hunter led 18,000 British southward from Transvaal and seized the temporary Orange Free State capital of Bethlehem in the northeastern part of the republic.

A number of Free Staters retreated southward to the Brandwater Basin against the Basutoland border, a fertile region of undulating pasture land bounded by mountains, whose few passes were easy to defend. Many of the Boers believed they could remain in the basin in safety. But De Wet saw the place not as a sanctuary but as a prison and, with President Steyn, led 2,500 men through one of the northern passes on July 5 before Hunter could seal it off.

The remaining Boers were supposed to break out the next day, but they got into a dispute over command and remained for two weeks. Meanwhile Hunter blocked most of the passes and the commander finally elected, Marthinus Prinsloo, surrendered 4,100 men on July 29, 1900, although 1,500 other Boers refused to quit and slipped out through a rugged eastern pass the Britons had not discovered.

Prinsloo's surrender ranked with Paardeberg as a Boer disaster, but the men who quit were the more faint-hearted. Similar defections of less-determined men were occurring elsewhere. The small minority that remained formed a hard core of resolute fighters. And these formidable men—the most skilled in surviving and the hardest to catch—were now being led by officers like De Wet who at last had turned to the Boers' great strengths, their mobility and vast knowledge of their country.

In early August 1900, the British learned the kind of war they were going to be required to fight. Lord Kitchener assembled 11,000 troops south of the Vaal River and 18,000 north of it to corner and defeat De Wet, who had established a strong position on the Vaal about twenty miles south of Potchefstroom. But trying to capture De Wet was like trying to grab quicksilver. De Wet slipped over a Vaal drift or ford on August 6 and moved into Transvaal. For the next eight days the British pursued him, sometimes close on his heels. But De Wet split his column and feinted as if he were going to double back into the Free State. This convinced Kitchener, who lost the scent. De Wet then raced north for the Gatsrand, a steep range of hills just northeast of Potchefstroom and about fifty miles southwest of Johannesburg.

Another British force came up to the railroad that ran a few miles west of the Gatsrand, certain De Wet would have to cross it to get deeper into Transvaal. Again the British missed. De Wet led his men across the railroad at night at a point the British were not occupying, then made speed for the Magaliesberg, a high, jagged, grey crescent of mountains running for a hundred miles west from Pretoria.

De Wet chose the pass that Lord Kitchener had ordered Lieutenant General Ian Hamilton to block. But Hamilton moved too slowly, and De Wet's last wagons had gone through when he came up. De Wet and his men were now safe, for the region was dominated by De la Rey and 7,000 Transvaalers and the British feared to enter it without mounting a large expedition.

By the end of August De Wet was back at his old post along the Vaal River, cutting the Central Railway and recruiting new soldiers. Once more the British took after him, but De Wet led them on a 500-mile chase and once more they failed.

The British found in these abortive campaigns that they

frequently became the hunted, for the Boers, who could usually outride them, captured British scouting parties with great regularity. The British also suffered because they insisted that their hunts, often involving half a dozen or more columns, must remain under central command. By the time the leader could be found to make a decision, the quarry had often flown.

Despite his failure to capture any of the major guerrilla leaders, Lord Roberts concluded that the war was over, and left for home in December 1900. In the interim, guerrilla warfare erupted over much of South Africa. Lord Kitchener, who took Roberts's place as commander, tried to stem the chaos, but without much success. The Boers attacked the railroads, ambushed convoys, recaptured isolated towns, and recruited openly in the country districts. The British had no control over large tracts of country. Indeed, they possessed only the territory they guarded: the main transportation arteries, mostly the railroads, and the cities. The guerrillas controlled the rest.

In November 1900, De Wet swept across the Free State, wrecked a stretch of railway, and forced 480 Britons to surrender at Dewetsdorp, 170 miles from his starting place.

This stunning success set off a flurry of Boer attacks at various points throughout December 1900. The month of horrors for the British commenced when De Wet invaded Cape Colony. But bad weather intervened and he turned back into the Free State. He was pursued by British forces who tried to hem him in against a line of hills north of Dewetsdorp. But De Wet easily avoided them. After splitting into small groups, his men disappeared into the veldt.

De la Rey in western Transvaal captured a convoy of 138 wagons and 1,800 oxen and inflicted 100 casualties on the troops guarding it. Soon afterward he and Christiaan F. Beyers fell on another convoy that its commander had laagered or camped at a poor site in a deep gorge at Nooitgedacht ("Never Expected") in the Magaliesberg, 40 miles west of Pretoria. Beyers's commando attacked the 300 British on the heights, killed, wounded or captured the lot, then sent heavy plunging fire directly down on the camp. With this, another Boer detachment attacked the camp itself, while De la Rey seized kopjes to the south, above the only route out of the gorge. But the Boers succumbed to plundering the captured wagons and about 1,000 British got away. Even so, they killed or captured 640 Britons.

Now James Hertzog in charge of one and and Pieter Kritzinger in command of another party invaded Cape Colony. They tore up railway tracks, destroyed communications, and ambushed small bodies of British. Hertzog got all the way to the coast 150 miles north of Cape Town, while Kritzinger turned south and penetrated almost to the ocean near Port Elizabeth. The spectacular invasion threw South Africa into a frenzy, infuriated the British, and greatly heartened the Boers. British forces chased after the two parties, but couldn't catch them.

De Wet, assembling 2,500 men, started for Cape Colony, hoping to join Hertzog. Kitchener tried to block him at two points, but De Wet got around him. However, heavy rains, and a screen of 15,000 men Kitchener threw up forced De Wet to give up the effort, and he and Hertzog crossed the Orange River on February 27, 1901. As they moved north, the elements of both commands melted away, the men going to ground or returning to their homes. The British had nothing left to chase.

In January 1901, Lord Kitchener commenced the program he hoped would bring the Boers to their knees but actually spelled the doom of the British attempt to win a decisive victory. He began the deliberate destruction of Boer farms, wherever they were found. Before the year was out, Britons burned an estimated 30,000 farmsteads and slaughtered 3.6 million sheep, the principal Boer livestock animal, as well as great numbers of horses, cattle, and goats. British Lieutenant David Miller wrote his mother regarding conditions in September 1901: "The country is now almost entirely laid waste. You can go for miles and miles—in fact you might march for weeks and weeks and see no sign of a living thing or a cultivated patch of land—nothing but burnt farms and desolation."[4]

An Australian wrote of one incident: "When within 800 yards of the farm we halted, and the infantry blazed a volley into the house; we broke open the place and went in. It was beautifully furnished and the officers got several things they could make use of. There was a lovely library—books of all descriptions, printed in Dutch and English. I secured a Bible, also a rifle, quite new. After getting all we wanted out of the house, our men put a charge under and blew it up. It seemed such a pity, it was a lovely house."[5]

The effects on the Boer families was often disastrous. Lieutenant Miller wrote: "The other day we discovered several families living in a great hole in a rock by the banks of the Vaal River. They are living entirely on fresh meat and

4. Farwell, 352–53, citing David S. Miller, *A Captain in the Gordons,* eds., Margaret and Helen Russell Miller (London: Sampson, Low, Marston & Co.), n.d., 107.

5. Ibid., 367–68.

mealie [maize] meal . . . [They] are, for the most part, in a frightful state of destitution—clothes made of blankets patched with bits of tablecloth or carpet."[6]

From this point on, until peace in May 1902, the war took on a new character. Its salient points were blockhouses to protect the railroads, concentration camps to hold thousands of Boer women, children, and old people, and a complex series of skirmishes by Boer raiding parties and British drives or sweeps to counter them.

The British destruction of Boer farms, upon which the people depended for their livelihood, caused immense privation and, in many cases, danger of starvation for many thousands of noncombatants. Although Kitchener advertised the burnings as a method to force the Boers to give up the fight, there was a scarcely disguised aim to take out his frustrations on the unarmed Afrikaner women and children, since he could not get at the soldiers.

The soldiers, he seemed to feel, should have the decency to meet the British in straightforward battle, where they could be shot down in a proper military manner. This has always been a characteristic response of the regular soldier against the guerrilla. The guerrilla will not fight by the regular army's rules. To the regular, this is unfair, not sporting. On July 8, 1901, Kitchener wrote in exasperation that the Boer parties would disperse when British troops appeared, "to reassemble in the same neighborhood when our men pass on. In this way they continue an obstinate resistance

6. Ibid., 366, citing Miller, *A Captain in the Gordons,* 102.

without retaining anything, or defending the smallest portion of this vast country."[7]

The British established fifty concentration camps in part to feed displaced persons and in part to punish those whose husbands or sons were fighting and force them to surrender.[8] But shortages of water and fresh food, inadequate sanitary conditions, little clothing or blankets, and exposure in the unshaded camps with only tents or reed huts for shelter were so great that the camps became deadly. British authorities only improved matters after an Englishwoman, Emily Hobhouse (1860–1935), visited the camps and announced their horrors to the world. Her report aroused intense anger in Britain and throughout the world. British leader Lloyd George charged that the government was like Herod, trying "to crush a little race by killing its young sons and daughters," while newspapers on the continent likewise accused the British of waging a war of extermination.[9] The uproar led the British government to appoint a Ladies Committee of six notable Englishwomen, who visited the camps and confirmed the conditions. Their report brought about im-

7. Ibid., 354, quoting W. Basil Worsfold, *Lord Milner's Work in South Africa* (New York: E. P. Dutton), 1906, 454.

8. Lord Kitchener sent a memorandum to all general officers on December 21, 1900, pointing out the advantage of bringing "all men, women and children and natives from the districts which the enemy's bands persistently occupy." This, he said, would be "the most effective method of limiting the endurance of the guerrillas." Kitchener also set up two classes in the concentration camps: families of those who had surrendered or were neutral, who would get preference in quarters and food, and families of active guerrillas, who would not. Because of questions raised in the House of Commons, the army, in late February and early March, 1901, discontinued this practice. See Farwell, 393, 399, 400; Pakenham, 523–24.

9. Farwell, 392–420; Pakenham, 533–49.

provements, but the stain on the British army and government remained.

In July and August 1901 Kitchener revealed he indeed was seeking to eliminate Boer opposition by extreme means. He proposed that all prisoners of war be transported outside South Africa and that their families be deported to join them. Then, he said, "there will be room for the British to colonize." The British cabinet, fearful of its implications, blocked the idea. Kitchener then proposed that the Boers themselves be required to pay the entire cost of the concentration camps by selling the property of men still fighting. "Let me take a strong line," Kitchener wrote the secretary for war, St. John Brodrick, "and I'll finish the war quickly." The cabinet scotched Kitchener's land-seizure recommendation as well.[10]

Nevertheless, Kitchener had hit upon virtually the only method that will defeat a people who refuse to bow to an invader: their eradication one way or another. Kitchener did not recommend that the Boers be killed, only driven from their homeland forever. Union General William Tecumseh Sherman, similarly frustrated by the bitter resistance of the South in the American Civil War, was not so comparatively humane. He wrote in 1864: "I am satisfied, and have been all the time, that the problem of war consists in the awful fact that the present class of men who rule the South must be killed outright rather than in the conquest of territory."[11]

However, most political leaders, like the men in the British cabinet, shrink from "final solutions." Whatever their private views, most leaders respond to the moral sense of

10. Pakenham, 545; Farwell, 399.

11. Earl Schenk Miers, *The General Who Marched to Hell* (New York: Dorset), 1990, 218.

humanity as a whole and recoil from such perversions. In this refusal, or unwillingness, of more powerful nations to take the final step to destroy utterly a weaker opponent lies the opportunity for weaker peoples to prevail.[12]

To protect their supply lines and hopefully to cripple the mobility of the Boers, the British built over 8,000 blockhouses, each able to deflect rifle fire, manned by seven men and located about 1,000 feet apart along the railways. Each was linked to the blockhouses on either side by heavy, high wire fences with tin cans affixed to make noise if Boers attempted to break through. At night armed black natives patrolled the line and armored trains were on call to come up anywhere the Boers attacked.

The system was extravagantly expensive and tied up about two-thirds of the 250,000 British troops in South Africa. But it guaranteed supplies and restricted the movements of the Boers, whose men on active service during the guerrilla period never exceeded 15,000 at any one time.[13] Even so, commandos could break through if determined, and the blockhouses did not bring the guerrillas to their knees, as many British officers liked to claim.

---

12. Not all peoples at all times possess this hesitancy. The Turks killed many thousands of Armenians in 1915. Adolf Hitler tried to destroy all the Jews and Gypsies in Europe in World War II. The Serbs in the former Yugoslavia embarked on a conscious policy of "ethnic cleansing" in the early 1990s to kill or drive out Moslems in those parts of Bosnia they wished to occupy. The Hutus massacred two-hundred thousand Tutsis in Rwanda in early 1994. There have been many other examples of genocide or forced evictions in world history. Nevertheless, such actions have always been seen by humanity as a whole as aberrations from an acceptable norm. Though other nations have often allowed such practices to go too far and on too long, they ultimately arouse such intense international opposition that they are stopped.

13. Belfield, 131; Pakenham, 543–4.

Kitchener concentrated his drives or hunts against the three most active Boer areas: northeastern Orange Free State, eastern Transvaal and northwestern Transvaal. A typical drive involved 5,000 to 10,000 men. The aim was to scour a region completely. Just like beaters in hunts for game back in Britain, soldiers walked or rode about ten yards apart and in line, trying to flush the Boers in front of them. The hunts seldom bagged many guerrillas, for the men and their horses broke through blockhouse lines or slipped through the net where gaps appeared. Nevertheless, Kitchener regularly sent reports on the numbers of "bags"—killed or captured—back to London, trying to prove that his system really was working.[14] His efforts bore a sad resemblance to the "body counts" of Communist soldiers that the American commander, William C. Westmoreland, fixed on during the Vietnam War to try to prove his system, too, was working.

The Boers used much ingenuity to strike convoys and isolated units. The actual effect on British strength was minimal, but the psychological damage was immense, both in the British army and at home.

One of the worst British defeats occurred in western Transvaal, fewer than three months before the end of the war. Lieutenant General Lord Methuen was leading 1,400 troops, many ill-trained, eastward from Vryburg. He planned to join Lieutenant Colonel H. M. Grenfell, who was advancing westward from Klerksdorp with 1,500 men. Together they would search out and destroy Koos De la Rey. But De la Rey watched Methuen's advance and on March 7, 1902, at Tweebosch, he struck with ' 100 men. First some Boers began harassing Methuen's rear guard. An hour later

14. Pakenham, 543.

other Boers threatened the column's right flank. Then De la Rey threw out three lines of skirmishers on the left rear of the column. Having distracted the British in three directions, he brought up his main force and it passed through the skirmishers at a gallop and charged straight for the British column, firing from the saddle. Most of the ill-trained Britons fled. Gunners with two cannons quickly unlimbered and started to fire, but the Boers shot them down and overran the pieces. Methuen gathered two more guns and 300 seasoned regulars who had not panicked for a last stand. It was quickly finished. The Boers overwhelmed the British, killing 68, wounding 121, including Methuen, and capturing over 600 all told. De la Rey sent Methuen to a British hospital under a flag of truce.[15]

John Y. F. Blake, an American who graduated from West Point in 1880 and who fought against the British, described how the Boers were able to survive. They divided into bands of 100 to 300 men. Each band operated as it pleased, but generally confined itself to its own district, though bands could come together quickly if the need arose. A band usually camped near a ruined farmstead where some grass remained for the horses to graze. If the British spotted them, the Boers would saddle up, dodge around the enemy, find another patch of grass, and try to get some sleep. They never put out sentries but everyone woke at 4 A.M., saddled his mount and prepared to fight at daylight. If the British appeared, the Boers would shoot a few from their horses and rush away to another district. If they didn't appear, the Boers would go back to sleep.

For meat, the Boers hunted antelope and other game,

15. Farwell, 389–91; Belfield, 136.

dried strips of it in the sun and made biltong, or they slaughtered cattle they kept with them. They also captured cattle
and army rations from the British. In season, they found
fresh vegetables and fruit growing wild. For grain, they
pulled out hidden plows in October, before the rainy season,
plowed some fields, planted maize or corn, and moved on.
The crops grew and the British couldn't burn many fields
because little grass grew up between the rows to serve as
tinder. The Boers stored the harvested maize among reeds
along rivers or in pits dug in the ground and covered.[16]

Taking into consideration the vast differences in climate
and technology, British operations in South Africa strongly
resembled those of the Americans in Vietnam over six decades later. That is, both powers marshaled seemingly overwhelming force and firepower, but spent only a fraction of it
in mobile forces searching for an elusive enemy. They were
compelled to expend much of their strength in defending
their bases or supply lines, since these were the most vulnerable to enemy attacks. In their efforts to find the guerrillas,
they alienated the people by attacks on their homes and
means of livelihood, while the native forces—Boers or Vietcong—enjoyed popular support because they were seeking
to protect the people.

By April 1902, the war had become a terrible burden for
both sides. Only the most determined Boers remained in the
ranks, while morale had fallen due to the losses of lives in the
concentration camps, the almost 25,000 Boer prisoners of
war held in camps abroad, and the destruction caused by
farm burning. For the British the outlook was equally bleak.

16. Belfield, 130–31.

The people at home were becoming increasingly restive and the war issue was certain to affect the next parliamentary election.

The Boers had produced a military stalemate, the first case in modern times where a guerrilla operation alone had achieved such results against the overwhelmingly superior forces of a major power.

Unlike the British high commissioner, Lord Alfred Milner, who wanted to make no concessions to the Boers, Kitchener possessed considerable political sense. He realized that the deadlock, while humiliating for Britain, was also a great burden for the Afrikaners. He couldn't defeat them, but they could not expel the British, nor prevent them from exploiting some of the region's resources. For example, about half of the uitlanders or foreign residents had returned and the Transvaal gold mines were working again, now under British supervision.

Kitchener concluded in March 1902, that the Boers might be willing to agree to peace under certain conditions. He was ready to grant some conditions in exchange for a face-saving political settlement that made it look like Britain had won. Kitchener engineered an extraordinary series of talks at Vereeniging, conducted under a British flag of truce, between the Boer factions. The proceedings were stormy but Louis Botha at last expressed the sense of all but the most die-hard: "Let us do what we can to save our people even if we must lose our independence."[17]

17. Ibid., 147. The British government tacitly acknowledged the achievements of the guerrillas by agreeing to negotiate only with them, thereby accepting that the guerrillas spoke for the Afrikaner people. The British ignored all other factions, including those Boers who had surrendered or had come over to the British side. When Lord Milner at a conference with the Boer leaders argued that the prisoners of war should be allowed to

The turning point came in subsequent talks with the British, when Kitchener assured Jan Smuts that the Boers would be granted responsible government in a short time if they would agree to peace.[18] This broke Boer opposition. In exchange for acknowledging the British sovereign, the Boers could expect to regain their effective independence. They also got other concessions: no war tax, no franchise for the black natives, Afrikaans as one of the official languages, and the Boers to retain their personal weapons. Britain granted self-government to Transvaal in 1906 and the Free State in 1907. The Boers immediately took over the governments. Most important was the concession regarding a native franchise, for this permitted the Boers, with the white British now becoming their allies, to hold all political power.[19] The final settlement came in 1910 when Britain conferred dominion status—that is, complete political control—on the 1,250,000 South African whites, giving them authority over the nearly 5,000,000 blacks, Coloreds (mixed-breeds), and Indians. In 1961 South Africa severed all ties with Britain and became a republic. The whites prevented the blacks from gaining equal rights until the first all-South African election in April 1994.

The British could advertise the peace of Vereeniging, which came May 31, 1902, as a victory, while the Boers received nearly all of the benefits of continued independence. They achieved this because of the guerrilla war.

vote on a proposed peace, Free State President M. T. Steyn asked what would happen if the prisoners voted to continue the war while the guerrillas in the commandos did not. The ensuing laughter silenced Milner. See Pakenham, 586; Farwell, 431.

18. Farwell, 436.

19. Klonis, 54–55. The British insisted that Afrikaner leaders in Cape Colony and Natal who had served with the Boers would stand trial for treason, but they promised none would be executed. See Farwell, 435–36.

SEVEN

War against a Vapor

T HE BRITISH and the rest of the world largely accepted the fiction that the peace of Vereeniging in May 1902 marked a victory of a conventional army over guerrillas who surrendered once they realized they were hopelessly outclassed and could not win.

Consequently, when a similar clash between the powerful and the feeble occurred in Arabia in World War I, no one looked for lessons in the Boer War. Rather, the principal intellectual figure of this confrontation—T. E. Lawrence or Lawrence of Arabia (1888–1935)—conceived a unique theory to rid Arabia of the Turks.[1] Seizing on Turkey's alliance with Germany, the Arabs rebelled against centuries of occupation by the Turks. Lawrence's theory grew out of his astute obser-

1. The basic source for Lawrence's Arabian campaign is his *Seven Pillars of Wisdom*, listed in Selected Bibliography (cited in notes following as Lawrence), and his condensation of the work: *Revolt in the Desert* (London: Jonathan Cape), 1927; (New York: George H. Doran), 1927. Works about him include David Garrett, ed., *The Letters of T. E. Lawrence* (London: Jonathan Cape), 1938; Robert Graves, *Lawrence and the Arabs* (London: Jonathan Cape), 1927; Basil H. Liddell Hart, *T. E. Lawrence* (London: Jonathan Cape), 1934; Anthony Nutting, *Lawrence of Arabia* (London: Hollis & Carter), 1961; Robert Payne, *Lawrence of Arabia—A Triumph* (New York: Pyramid Books), 1963.

vations of the conditions and peoples he encountered in Arabia. Lawrence knew little about the Boer War and his system apparently owed nothing to the lessons taught by it.

Yet Lawrence's solution demonstrated decided parallels with Boer methods. Most especially Lawrence, like the Boers, arrived at the fundamental key to guerrilla success: strike at enemy weakness and avoid enemy strength.

Lawrence was a young intelligence lieutenant in Cairo. After graduating from Oxford University in 1910 with an honors degree in history, Lawrence spent several years in Middle Eastern archeological digs and acquired a firm knowledge of the Arabic language.

For more than two and a half years, the British army under General Sir Archibald Murray had accomplished little against a combined Turkish and German force, which faced the British from Gaza to Beersheba in the Sinai desert and threatened the Suez Canal. As a means of distracting the Turks, whose empire included Arabia and the Moslem holy cities of Medina and Mecca, the British instigated the Arab Revolt on June 10, 1916. Its leader was Hussein, sharif of Mecca and paramount chief of the Hejaz region of western Arabia along the Red Sea.

Hussein captured Mecca, but his forces, composed of Bedouin tribesmen and commanded by his sons Feisal, Ali, and Abdullah, were poorly organized and equipped, and unable to seize Medina. The Turks maintained their hold because of the supplies delivered on the Hejaz Railway, which ran down to Medina from Damascus, Syria.

Lawrence got permission to visit Hussein in October 1916 with the British diplomat, Ronald Storrs. Lawrence was impressed only with Hussein's son, Feisal. Lawrence saw that Feisal possessed the qualities to arouse the dormant

spirit of Arab nationalism, and might convince the fiercely
independent Bedouin tribes to work toward a common goal
of winning a war of liberation.

Lawrence applied his mind to the essential strategic problem the Turks faced in Arabia and how the disparate, competitive tribes best could exploit this problem. He saw what
the British military leadership in Cairo did not see: that the
Hejaz Railway was the Achilles' heel of the Turks and could
be used against them.

The British leaders saw merely that the railroad was the
only means of supply for the Medina garrison. Therefore,
they reasoned, the Bedouins should come out of their natural
environment, the Arabian Desert—through which much of
the railway ran—and cut the line. To keep the line cut the
Arabs would have to fight a stand-up battle against heavy
Turkish arms. If the Arabs won, the Turks would be forced
to abandon Medina and the Hejaz. Thus the British wanted
the Arabs to employ the conventional way of making military decisions.

Lawrence recognized three fallacies in the argument: (1)
the Arabs must acquire large numbers of heavy weapons that
could meet Turkish arms on an equal basis, and would have
to be trained in their use, and the British were unlikely to
provide weapons or training, (2) the Arabs had no generals
skilled in conventional war and their tribal structure ren-
dered them incapable of the military discipline and organization necessary to confront the Turks in open battle, and (3)
if the 25,000 Turks in the Medina garrison moved north,
they could reinforce the Turkish-German army in the Sinai,
mount a greater threat to the Suez Canal, and make it even
more difficult for the British.

Lawrence came up with a far more subtle and suitable

plan to stymie the Turks in Arabia and assist the British army in driving into Palestine and forcing the Turkish empire to quit the war. He proposed that the railway be sabotaged regularly but that it be kept barely open, just capable of feeding the Turks at Medina. This would force the Turks to devote most of their strength to defending the line, leaving little energy for other actions. He was confident the Turks would remain in Medina as long as possible. As Moslems, their possession of the holy city confirmed their legitimacy as the sovereign power. Thus, the Turks holding Medina would become as ineffective in fighting the British as if they were lodged in a prisoner-of-war camp.

Lawrence also saw that the Arabs, with light arms and few more skills than they already possessed as desert mounted men, could break the railway, disappear rapidly into the desert, and reappear at some other place, repeatedly. As had happened in South Africa, this would create a military stalemate that the occupying power over time could not endure. Lawrence's was a classic recipe for guerrilla warfare, adapted to the peculiar circumstances of the Turkish occupation and the Arabian Desert.

If the Arabs had come "like an army with banners," the Turks would have defended Arabia by a trench line, Lawrence wrote. "But suppose," he went on, "we were an influence, an idea, a thing intangible, invulnerable, without front or back, drifting about like a gas?"

In comparison with the Bedouin who "might be a vapor, blowing where he listed," conventional armies, Lawrence wrote, are "like plants, immobile, firm-rooted, nourished through long stems to the head."[2] That is, an invading or occupying army can only survive if it is constantly replen-

2. Lawrence, 192.

ished with food, ammunition, and other supplies delivered from a distant source, usually the army's homeland. This supply line is the army's umbilical cord. If it is cut, the army withers away. On the other hand a guerrilla army can move at will in any direction, for long periods, more or less independently of its supplies, since it carries the small amounts of ammunition it needs and usually takes along its food as well, or can get more from friendly natives.

Lawrence thus outlined a condition that has bedeviled all conventional armies at all times when they are confronted with an enemy who refuses to encounter them directly "like an army with banners." When an enemy moves away from an army's power, toward its weakness, he has the capability of deadlocking the ordinary army, denying it victory, even if he can't destroy it.

For example, in 329 B.C. Alexander the Great faced serious guerrilla warfare in the Persian satrapies of Bactria and Sogdiana (roughly present-day Afghanistan and the Turkestan region on both sides of the Amu Darya or Oxus and the Syr Darya or Jaxartes rivers). In this theater Alexander encountered a people's war of mounted guerrillas who would suddenly attack his rear or shoot down from inaccessible crags. When pursued, they would vanish into the Turkomen steppes. Pursuit therefore forced Alexander's army to move steadily away from its supplies, reducing its mobility, lengthening its logistical tail, and limiting the potential reach of its power. Although Alexander subdued the region, he never really conquered the people, and, fearing disaster from Scythian horse-archers, made no attempt to penetrate beyond the Jaxartes permanently.[3]

3. J. F. C. Fuller, *The Generalship of Alexander the Great* (New Brunswick, N.J.: Rutgers University Press), 1960; (New York: Da Capo), 1989, 117, 234–45.

During the Second Punic War (219–202 B.C.) the Roman dictator Quintus Fabius Maximus prevented Hannibal from conquering Italy with similar semiguerrilla "Fabian" tactics used by the Roman army itself. The Romans had poor cavalry, and were unable to meet the Carthaginians on the plains where Hannibal's superb cavalry made him invincible. To avoid defeat, Fabius remained in the hills, where cavalry was less effective, and struck at Carthaginian outposts, patrols, and supply lines. None of these blows was decisive, but together they prevented Hannibal from achieving victory and kept Rome's allies from going over to the Carthaginian side.

Since the Hejaz Railway ran through the Arabian Desert, Lawrence saw that the Bedouin could approach almost any point along it with impunity, and then vanish once more into the desert's deep reaches. This left the Turks in the military position of having "all flanks and no front."[4] It was an insoluble dilemma for the Turks, and most armies face similar problems when they occupy a conquered land.

Lawrence saw that conventional wars are wars of contact, with both sides striving to touch the other to avoid tactical surprise. "Ours," Lawrence wrote, "should be a war of detachment. We were to contain the enemy by the silent threat of a vast unknown desert, not disclosing ourselves until we attacked. The attack might be nominal, directed not against him, but against his stuff; so it would not seek either his strength or his weakness, but his most accessible material. In railway cutting it would be usually an empty stretch of rail; and the more empty, the greater the tactical success. . . . Many Turks on our front had no chance all the war to fire on us, and we were never on the defensive except by accident or in error."[5]

4. Lawrence, 225.
5. Ibid., 194.

Lawrence said that "we had nothing material to lose, so our best line was to defend nothing and to shoot nothing. Our cards were speed and time, not hitting power. The invention of bully beef had profited us more than the invention of gunpowder, but gave us strategical rather than tactical strength, since in Arabia range was more than force, space greater than the power of armies."[6]

Lawrence concluded that the Arab Revolt

had an unassailable base, guarded not only from attack, but from the fear of attack. It had a sophisticated alien enemy, disposed as an army of occupation in an area greater than could be dominated effectively from fortified posts. It had a friendly population, of which some two in a hundred were active, and the rest quietly sympathetic to the point of not betraying the movements of the minority. The active rebels had the virtues of secrecy and self-control, and the qualities of speed, endurance and independence of arteries of supply. They had technical equipment enough to paralyze the enemy's communications.[7]

Lawrence began to take over direction of the Arab Revolt after Bedouin tribesmen under Prince Feisal almost allowed the Turks to seize the Red Sea port of Yenbo, about 200 miles north of Jidda. The British were using Yenbo to supply the Arabs. Snipers in the hills gave way rapidly to the first major Turkish assault, and the Turks drove Feisal's 5,000-man camel corps into the town. Only salvos from hastily concentrated British warships forced the Turks to draw off.[8]

Lawrence talked Feisal into moving 200 miles farther north to the port of Wejh (Al Wagh), which would give a

6. Ibid., 196.
7. Ibid.
8. Asprey, vol. 1, 282–4.

base closer to Suez, making it easier for the British to bring in supplies. Despite an arduous march through the desert, Feisal's men arrived at Wejh after a seaborne attack by a small force of Arab infantry and British marines had seized the port, with the help of six British warships.

The Turks had insufficient mobility to pursue such far-ranging groups of Arabs, aided by British sea power, and fell back on Medina, where half the force guarded the city and the remainder protected the railway.

Lawrence now conceived of seizing the port of Aqaba, at the northern end of the Red Sea, 250 air miles northwest of Wejh. This would be an ideal supply base from which to operate guerrillas against the railway. Instead of marching directly on Aqaba, however, Lawrence induced Feisal's men to take a long and extremely hazardous roundabout 800-mile journey through deserts considered to be impassable. The Arabs descended on the rear of the port on July 6, 1917, achieving complete surprise and total success.

The capture of Aqaba came only a few days after General Sir Edmund Allenby (1861–1936) arrived at Cairo to replace Murray as supreme commander. Shortly afterward, Lawrence rode across the Sinai desert to Cairo. Allenby was impressed with Lawrence's feat and received him in his flowing Arab robes, promoted him to major, and sent him back to guide the Arab Revolt.

Allenby wanted Lawrence to cut the Hejaz Railway permanently but Lawrence argued that this would force the Turks to abandon Medina. "The Turks were harmless there," he wrote. "We wanted them to stay at Medina, and every other distant place, in the largest numbers." Lawrence was convinced that "the factor of food" would confine the Turk to the railway and "pride in his imperial heritage" would keep him in Medina. "But he was welcome to the Hejaz Railway. . . . so long as he gave us the other nine-hundred and ninety-nine thousandths of the Arab world."[9]

Lawrence operated under three conditions, all almost directly contrary to ordinary army doctrine: (1) irregulars would not attack places like cities or major fortifications, and therefore were incapable of forcing a decision, (2) they were as unable to defend a line or point as they were to attack it, and (3) their virtue lay in depth, not in face.

Lawrence and Arab parties now commenced a series of blows against the railway, tearing up track, blowing up culverts, and occasionally stopping and assaulting trains. The Turks never knew where the Arabs would strike. For their mobility and mastery of the desert permitted them to move almost at will and for vast distances.

The Bedouins, Lawrence concluded, had to extend their front to its maximum, "to impose on the Turks the longest possible passive defense, since that was, materially, their most costly form of war. . . . We could develop a highly mobile, highly equipped striking force of the smallest size, and use it successively at distributed points of the Turkish line, to make them strengthen their posts [along the railway]. . . . This would be a shortcut to success."[10]

Lawrence summed up his tactics as follows:

Our operations . . . should be like naval war, in mobility, in ubiquity, independence of bases and communications, ignoring of ground features, of strategic areas, of fixed directions, of fixed points. He who commands the sea is at great liberty, and may take as much or as little of the war as he will. And we commanded the desert. Camel raiding parties, self-contained like ships, might

9. Lawrence, 225.
10. Ibid., 224.

cruise confidently along the enemy's cultivation-frontier, sure of an unhindered retreat into their desert element, which the Turks could not explore. . . . Our tactics should be tip and run: not pushes, but strokes. We should never try to improve an advantage. We should use the smallest force in the quickest time at the farthest place.[11]

In pursuit of these tactics in the harsh Arabian Desert, Lawrence relied on the camel, which he called "that intricate, prodigious piece of nature." When he embarked on a raid, each team member threw a 45-pound sack of flour over his riding saddle. This gave the man six weeks of food, which equaled a capacity for 1,000 miles of movement, out and back. Men carried no more than a pint of water apiece. This was because the camels had to drink, "and there was no gain," Lawrence wrote, "in making ourselves richer than our mounts." Men drank fully at every well and carried a drink for only a single dry day. In summer camels could go 250 miles after watering, or three days of vigorous march. Since wells were seldom 100 miles apart, the pint reserve for the men was latitude enough. The parties carried little forage for the camels, since they could normally find some plants to eat along the way.

Lawrence insisted on simple, but effective, weapons for raiders. They carried British army rifles, but relied on Hotchkiss or Lewis light automatic machine guns, which provided much greater firepower. Lawrence kept the men deliberately ignorant of the mechanism of these guns, in order for them not to waste speed in action in efforts at repair. "Ours were battles of minutes," Lawrence wrote, "fought at eighteen miles an hour. If a gun jammed, the gunner must throw it aside and go in with his rifle."

11. Ibid., 224, 337.

The teams evolved special methods with dynamite that permitted them to demolish a track or culvert with economy, safety, and speed.[12]

Arab attacks contributed materially to the success of the British offensives of October 1917 which breached the Turko-German Gaza-Beersheba line, and of September 1918 which cracked the new line north of Jerusalem. In this final campaign, which resulted in defeat of Turkey and its withdrawal from the war on October 31, 1918, Lawrence's Arabs broke the Turkish railway at Deraa, east of the Jordan River valley, and shut off supplies by way of the branch line into Palestine.

General Allenby used the Arabs and a feigned attack by British troops into the Jordan valley to convince Turkish commanders that the main blow was aimed in that direction. Actually Allenby broke the enemy line along the Mediterranean near Jaffa and rushed a cavalry corps up the Plain of Sharon to seize the heights of Mount Carmel and turn east, cutting off the retreat of all enemy armies in Palestine.

The principal aim of Lawrence's strike at Deraa was to keep the enemy's command intent on the trans-Jordan front just as the real attack erupted on the coast on the night of September 18. Allenby, who recognized the psychological value of a guerrilla strike against an unexpected point at a critical time, told Lawrence: "Three men and a boy with pistols in front of Deraa on September 16 would fill his conception; would be better than thousands a week before or a week after."[13]

Because the Arab Revolt was intimately tied in with the British war against Turkey, it's impossible to determine

12. Ibid., 337–8.
13. Ibid., 539.

whether it alone would have forced the Turks to withdraw from all lands in the Middle East they occupied where Arabic was spoken. These included, in addition to the western Arabian peninsula, the regions that became Syria, Lebanon, Iraq, Jordan, and Palestine after the war. But Arab strikes held down many thousands of Turkish soldiers and demonstrated that guerrilla warfare could be applied as well in desert lands as in the steppes of South Africa.

EIGHT

Mao Zedong: Strike Enemy Weakness

Mao zedong brought Communism to China in large measure because he understood that weak forces can neutralize strong forces by indirect means.

Mao adapted fundamental principles of war to counter the greatly superior power of Nationalist Chinese government forces and the Japanese army in China in the 1920s and 1930s. This led to his victory. However, Mao's system by no means is limited to a particular time and place. It was the foundation for the Communist success in Vietnam, and it can have application today in insurgencies and in wars against an invading power anywhere. Mao solved the major problems that inferior forces encounter in such circumstances in overcoming superior military power.

Lawrence of Arabia did the same thing. There is no indication that Lawrence influenced Mao. Yet Mao's and Lawrence's concepts are parallel. This is no accident. Great commanders when confronted with similar challenges come up with similar solutions. Consequently the analogies between Mao and Lawrence transcend the vastly different physical and social environments faced by the Bedouins and the Chinese.

One of the parallels is that Lawrence and Mao recognized it is destructive to throw weakly armed forces directly against conventional armies with heavy weapons and air power. Instead, both came to the dictum first recorded in the fifth century B. C. by the Chinese strategist Sun Tzu: "The way to avoid what is strong is to strike what is weak."[1] Both saw that weak forces had to deliver quick, hard, and unexpected blows against a vulnerable, but weakly defended, enemy point, and just as quickly disappear before overwhelming conventional power could be marshaled against them.

Mao adopted another Sun Tzu dictum—that a commander should strike at an important point the enemy has to defend. But, unlike countless unimaginative generals over the ages who have attacked the objective directly in front of them, Sun Tzu called for striking a point that is important to the enemy but one he does not expect to be attacked. Such a goal is almost certain to be weakly defended or not at all. Sun Tzu wrote: "You may advance and be absolutely irresistible if you make for the enemy's weak points."[2] To open a way to these weak points, Sun Tzu wrote that the general must deceive the enemy: "Make an uproar in the east, strike in the west." Striking enemy weak points and deception are the essence of his indirect strategy, and can succeed against conventional armies.

A conventional army commander most often sees the striking elements of the enemy army as his primary objective. Historically, this has led to massive direct clashes between

1. Sun Tzu, II, 29.
2. Ibid., 26.

armies on battlefields, like Waterloo in 1815 or the Battle of the Bulge in late 1944.

But Mao Zedong saw other objectives than the heart of the enemy army's offensive power. These objectives were the enemy's supply lines, rear bases, and isolated enemy detachments, outposts or garrisons. If Mao could strike at these objectives, while avoiding the enemy's main strength, he could force the enemy to defend them. This would give the initiative to Mao's weaker force and compel the stronger enemy to concentrate most of his strength in guarding his rear and his lines of communication and supply.

Recognizing that the enemy's rear is his most vulnerable target, Mao abandoned any attempt to defend a front or main line of resistance. This obliged him to give up orthodox warfare in which one army directly confronts another and attempts to destroy it. In Mao's system, orthodox war could only come at the final stage just prior to victory, after the enemy had been weakened and demoralized. To prepare for this culminating stage, he adopted indirect warfare, essentially guerrilla or semi-guerrilla in its operation, that avoided a straightforward challenge to the enemy's main strength. This turned the enemy rear into the guerrilla's area of operation—in effect, the guerrilla's front. Mao's system not only distracted the enemy, but solved the Reds' logistical problems as well: the enemy became the guerrilla's principal source of weapons, equipment, and ammunition.

As Lawrence had concluded in Arabia, Mao saw that his best strategy was to defend nothing. This allowed his forces to conceal their weakness—lack of hitting power—and exploit their strength: the capacity to move at speed and appear at the time and place of their choosing, and thereby surprise the enemy.

The Nationalist or Kuomintang (KMT) party got valuable aid from the Soviet Union upon forming an alliance in 1922 with Premier Joseph Stalin. But the KMT leader Chiang Kai-shek harbored right-wing convictions and feared a Communist takeover of the KMT. When Chiang won southern and central China in 1927, he exploited his new strength, broke his alliance with the Communists, and killed all Communists he could find. The surviving Communists realized they must develop a military force to challenge the KMT. But most Communists, following doctrinaire Marxist ideas, believed that the people would rise up in mass and destroy the existing regime.

Mao Zedong saw a different solution. He developed his theories without benefit of formal military training. And they sprang from failure. After the massacres, the Red leadership ordered "autumn harvest" uprisings in 1927 in Hubei and Hunan provinces. The leaders insisted that peasants and workers alone, motivated mostly by their enthusiasm for reform and virtually without weapons, could overthrow the existing society.

Mao led several ill-organized forces against the Hunanese capital of Changsha and vicinity, but they failed miserably and Kuomintang troops captured Mao himself. Although he escaped and hid in tall grass, all he could do was retreat with about a thousand survivors to a famous bandit bastion, Jinggang shan, in the Luoxiao Mountains dividing Hunan and Jiangxi provinces in southeast China. A year later they moved to the vicinity of Ruijin, 120 miles southeast in the Wuyi Mountains on the Jiangxi-Fujian border. There Mao set up a small "central soviet" and prepared to test his radical theories.

Mao was convinced that peasants and workers would not

bring about the downfall of the Nationalists and believed this had been confirmed in the autumn harvest uprisings. The masses, he said, could not go up against KMT troops armed with machine guns and cannon. Only reliable, disciplined, effective Red armies, organized both as regular forces and guerrillas, could fight the well-armed Kuomintang armies and win.

Mao therefore recognized a prerequisite of successful guerrilla warfare: support of the people. Mao tested his theory in the small soviet around Ruijin, where he divided confiscated landlords' property among the peasants, set up schools, eliminated high interest rates on loans, and reduced high local taxes. In these ways he gained peasant devotion.

He preached that the greatest danger was from the landlord class that owned much of the farmland and imposed heavy taxes on the peasants and exploited them with excessive rents and exorbitant interest rates on loans. To gain mass support, Mao called for ousting the landlords and dividing farmland equitably among the peasants. By promising to improve the farmer's lot, Mao taught, the army he planned to build would gain the loyalty of the people.

Mao therefore recognized a prerequisite of successful guerrilla warfare: support of the people. Mao tested his theory in the small soviet around Ruijin, where he divided confiscated landlords' property among the peasants, set up schools, eliminated high interest rates on loans, and reduced high local taxes. In these ways he gained peasant devotion.

At the same time Mao, with the help of a Communist soldier, Zhu De, created a new army with a new sort of soldier. From the start, the political role of the army and its soldiers was as important as their military role. In 1927 Mao had summed up the essence of his revolutionary theory in his most famous aphorism: "We must be aware that political power grows out of the barrel of a gun." Military operations were necessary, yet were only the means to the goal of revolutionary change. Consequently, the army's first task was to convert the people to the idea of revolution. The war would be decided by moral factors, not weapons.

The army was voluntary. Only persons dedicated and willing to fight could bear the hardships of campaigning, Mao wrote. The army also was as democratic as a hierarchical command structure can be. Mao discouraged the traditional caste system in most armies, recruiting troop leaders from the ranks, and forming no distinct officers corps, the Red political cadres serving this leadership function. Unlike the custom in China at the time, leaders treated soldiers kindly, lived with them in the same spartan quarters, ate the same food, and wore the same uniform. Officers were elected by the soldiers and did not bear military ranks, but were addressed by their job titles, such as "comrade platoon leader," or "comrade company commander."

The Red cadres forbade soldiers seizing food or property from the peasants and punished rape, robbery, and violence harshly. They also encouraged soldiers to solve various everyday problems. This led to extensive precombat briefings of the rank and file about the tactical situation and battle plans, a practice virtually unheard of in other armies, whose leaders seldom trust their common soldiers. The briefings contributed greatly to the soldiers' sense of responsibility to work as part of a larger organization possessing an elevated, society-altering goal. They became active participants, not mute followers of orders.

The army consisted of both regular forces and guerrilla units. Although poorly armed, it commanded great strength.

The basic unit was a combat group or team, usually of three men. The team members had the duty to look out for each other. This mutual dependence helped to solve the problem, present in all armies, of getting the individual soldier actually to fight. It rested on the idea that camaraderie is good for morale, while example and intimate face-to-face relationships condition social behavior. Three teams usually made up a squad. Thus, the squad leader had only three men to control, increasing efficiency greatly.

Over a four-year period, Chiang Kai-shek tried to destroy Mao Zedong and his soviet. In defending against these successive "bandit-suppression" drives, Mao developed guerrilla tactics that were consistently successful, despite the fact that KMT forces were always greatly superior in numbers and weapons.

In Chiang's first campaign, December 1930, Chiang attempted to drive into the soviet area from several directions with 100,000 soldiers, well-equipped with artillery and fighter-bombers. His aim was to corner the 40,000 Communist troops, many who had no weapons at all, and force them into a stand-up battle, in which they would be destroyed.

Mao and Zhu De countered this annihilation strategy by a combination of secret, highly mobile movements, mostly at night, of the Red regular army columns combined with guerrilla strikes at the rear of the KMT forces. The regular Communist units withdrew before Kuomintang troops, pulling them farther and farther into the region.

Using spies from local-defense paramilitary groups in the villages, the Communists kept track of exactly where the KMT forces were. When they discovered a weak or ill-led force, they attempted to lure it into difficult terrain by minor provocations. If the Communists succeeded in exhausting and isolating the force, they concentrated troops and stormed the unit with overwhelming odds, ten-to-one, if possible. The aim was complete destruction. Mao wrote: "Injuring all of a man's fingers is not as effective as chopping off one of them, and routing ten enemy divisions is not as effective as annihilating one of them."[3]

Chiang's first "extermination campaign" failed. In early 1931 he placed one of his most reliable generals, He Yingqin, in command of his second campaign, sending 200,000 troops of regional warlords into the central soviet. Mao's forces had declined to about 30,000. However, He Yingqin repeated the same plan of the first campaign, moving ponderously into Communist areas by seven routes. Mao repeated his tactics and by May, 1931, had won again, capturing 20,000 Kuomintang rifles.

In July 1931, Chiang brought in 100,000 of his own troops and 200,000 warlord soldiers for his third campaign. Chiang was sure his own well-equipped soldiers would make short work of the Communists. Since 1927, Chiang had employed German advisers to train his army. But the German officers were experts in stand-up fights between European field armies, and Mao Zedong's semi-guerrilla warfare called for different tactics, training, and orientation.

Chiang planned to drive straight into the soviet, hoping to take the region by storm, squeezing the Communists into a corner and forcing them to stand up and fight. Mao's forces, still about 30,000 men, were resting in the Wuyi Mountains. To get into position, Mao moved by forced marches to an assembly point about thirty-five miles north-

3. Nigel de Lee in Pimlott, 35–36.

west of Ruijin. Mao hoped to move northward, slip around behind the Nationalist forces, and strike at isolated units from the rear. But KMT observers detected the movement and Chiang rushed two divisions to block them. To avoid entrapment, Mao fell back to the south, then moved northeast under cover of night through a thirteen-mile gap between two KMT groups. This again would put the Communists into the rear of several advancing Kuomintang divisions. But Chiang might locate them and concentrate his army around them.

However, Mao got clean through the KMT forces without being detected and on two successive days concentrated against separated KMT divisions and sent them reeling. The Red Army now moved even farther east and defeated another Kuomintang division. But Chiang ordered all his forces to mass against the now-pinpointed Communists and seek a battle of annihilation.

Mao's peasant spy network gave him word of the movement, and, following his dictum never to stand up against a stronger force, he ordered immediate retreat westward at all speed. His scouts found a seven-mile gap in high mountains between KMT forces, and the Red Army slipped through it and reassembled northwest of Ruijin. There the soldiers collapsed in exhaustion.

When Chiang's forces, weary, discouraged and hungry after several days of searching for the Communists in vain, discovered that the quarry had flown, they moved out of the soviet in late September, 1931.

Because of preoccupation with Japan, which occupied Manchuria in 1931, Chiang did not mount his fourth "bandit-suppression" campaign against Mao until January, 1933. This effort, like the previous ones, ended in failure.

The Communist Party's urban-based leadership, which had never been happy with Mao's rural soviet, emphasis on peasants, and guerrilla tactics, responded to a renewed KMT offensive in 1934 with orders that the Red Army meet the Nationalist forces head to head, challenging them in direct combat. The result was disaster. Many in the Communist forces were killed or wounded, and Chiang's troops sealed off the soviet and began its systematic destruction. This led, in October 1934, to the Communists' abandonment of the soviet and the Long March, which ended a year later when a fragment of the army arrived in the Yan'an region of northern Shaanxi province in north China next to Inner Mongolia. During the Long March, Mao showed ways to avoid the pursuing Nationalists and saved the Red Army from destruction. As a result, he took over effective control of the Communist movement in China.

In 1937, Japanese aggression against China turned into a full-scale war. The Japanese spread over much of northern and central China. To create internal Chinese unity, Chiang agreed to form a united front with the Communists. Although the alliance was in name only, the two sides cooperated in some degree against the common enemy.

To advise the Chinese on fighting the Japanese, Mao published *Guerrilla Warfare* in 1937.[4] It was the first systematic study of the subject and is remarkable for two reasons: (1) it summarized the lessons Mao had learned in his war of insurgency against the Nationalists, and (2) showed how the

4. Samuel B. Griffith translated Mao's work in 1940. Praeger Publishers, New York, published the work in 1961, with an introduction by Griffith, under the title *Mao Tse-tung on Guerrilla Warfare*. In the notes following it is cited as Mao Zedong.

same techniques could be used against a foreign invader, in this case Japan.

Scholars have largely ignored this latter message and have seen Mao's study mostly as the bible of insurgency warfare. The majority of analysts have viewed Mao's methods as primarily designed to assist a radical minority within a country to mount and sustain an internal rebellion aimed at violent revolution against an existing government. They have cited the Vietnam War as the leading example: that the Vietnamese Communists, who employed Mao's theory, were an insurgent minority rebelling against the established government of Vietnam.

Yet the Vietnamese Communists were able to gain wide popular support because their primary aim was to achieve national independence by ousting invading imperialists—first France and then the United States. This was the identical goal of the Chinese against the Japanese. From the point of view of the Chinese and of the Vietnamese Communists, the domestic governments supporting the imperialist invaders were puppets. To them their war was not an internal struggle between factions but a war to repel external aggressors.

In this light, Mao Zedong's 1937 book has immense significance today for weaker countries that are forced to conduct wars against powerful aggressor states. For Mao explains how invaders can be hobbled, not by fighting the invaders' military power directly, but by avoiding this power and striking at their weaknesses.

In the 1930s, the Nationalists possessed far better arms than the Communists, but remained much inferior to the Japanese, whose industries were able to supply the army with the most modern equipment. Against Japanese firepower, Chinese armies invariably melted. As a consequence, Japanese armies occupied all of north China, much of central China, and all China's major ports. But here the Japanese armies had to stop. Because they feared an attack from the Soviet Union, the Japanese had to keep large forces in the home islands and on guard in Manchuria, and could spare only a million fighting men for China. These were insufficient to occupy the vast outer reaches of the country.

Stymied, the Japanese tried to conclude a peace treaty with Chiang Kai-shek. But he knew any agreement with Japan would turn the country into an exploited colony. Thus no peace treaty was possible. Nevertheless, the KMT armies were unable to meet Japanese forces on even terms and were virtually useless militarily. A stalemate developed, but it benefited Japan, not China, because the Japanese held China's most productive economic regions and only the Chinese Communists were interested in mounting a guerrilla war in their rear.

Nevertheless, Mao Zedong found a way to counter Japanese power—and pointed the way for any weaker country to do the same. His book was largely aimed at motivating the KMT to develop a guerrilla program as a way to damage, distract, and hobble the Japanese. But he always held that no guerrilla force, however effective, alone could win a war against a conventional army.

Mao maintained that the weaker power could gain in strength through guerrilla war while the invading power declined. In time, a turning point would come and the invaded country could field regular armies that could meet the invaders on even terms and defeat them.

This time never came against the Japanese. The United States defeated Japan and forced it to relinquish its conquests in 1945. Although Communist guerrillas occupied rural north China, leaving only the cities and the rail lines under Japanese control, the Nationalists failed to set up a guerrilla program in other parts of the Japanese rear. Therefore, Mao's theory was never fully tested against the invader.

However, Mao did use his theory against Nationalists in the Chinese Civil War, which erupted in 1946. He started with extensive guerrilla warfare. As his guerrillas succeeded and captured more and more military equipment from KMT armies, Mao expanded his regular field armies. These armies defeated KMT forces and seized the mainland by 1949, forcing Chiang and die-hard survivors to flee to Taiwan.

In Vietnam, the Communist leader Ho Chi Minh and his great military commander, Vo Nguyen Giap, also proved the legitimacy of Mao's theory by using it to succeed in wars against France and the United States.

Let us now examine Mao Zedong's theory. Its primary aim is to direct small but frequent, vicious attacks against enemy towns, bases, depots, and lines of communications or supply. This will force the enemy to disperse his forces widely and in small detachments to protect these vital points. Even guarded, these objectives remain vulnerable, because the enemy can't predict which ones the guerrillas will attack. Such uncertainty will demoralize the enemy, lead to his decline, and open the way finally for regular domestic forces, organized in orthodox armies, to challenge the invader and defeat him.[5]

5. Nigel de Lee in Pimlott, 48. In an insurgent war, or an internal "war of liberation" against a domestic government, such as he led against the Nationalists, Mao postulated a three-phase contest. In phase one, political teams go into villages, arouse the people, and establish bases for revolt. In phase two, guerrilla forces undertake active operations against enemy troops in a wider contested zone, seeking to expand the size of the liber-

In Manchuria in the early stages of the Chinese Civil War, Chiang Kai-shek, faced with Communist guerrilla attacks at widely separated points, refused to disperse his forces. Instead, he concentrated them in a few cities. Chiang was trying to avoid being defeated piecemeal by attacks on isolated detachments. But his strategy was no solution. It immobilized his armies and allowed the Communists to cut their supply lines, besiege the cities, and starve the garrisons into submission.[6]

Mao's system won't result in quick victory, but in protracted war. It will result ultimately in the defeat of the enemy or his exhaustion with the strain, and his withdrawal. The system's great strength, as Mao wrote, is that it offers "a weapon that a nation inferior in arms and military equipment may employ against a more powerful aggressor nation."[7]

Since a country engaged in guerrilla warfare abandons the concept of a line of resistance, the enemy can move

ated bases. Once the enemy is sufficiently weakened and insurgent forces strengthened, revolutionaries in phase three transform a significant part of the guerrilla units into orthodox military forces capable of challenging the enemy's regular armies in stand-up battles, leading to their defeat and takeover of the state by the revolutionaries. Revolutionaries can be deluded by successes in phase two into moving to phase three prematurely. When this happens and defeat occurs, revolutionaries must move back to phase two, and possibly to phase one. In wars against a foreign invader, the people do not have to be converted to revolutionary ideology. Hence phase one is unnecessary and guerrilla forces can be organized among the population at large. Even so, the transition to phase three, or ordinary operations by regular field armies, still must come only after phase two, or guerrilla operations, have weakened the enemy sufficiently. See ibid., 46–47; Mao Zedong, 20–22, 47–48.

6. An invader coming from overseas can avoid having his supplies shut off by establishing "beachheads" on the shore which can be supported by ships. However, this strategy also is not a solution, since it would paralyze the invader and leave the rest of the country in enemy hands.

7. Mao Zedong, 42, 67.

throughout the country's entire territory. Therefore, everywhere is in the rear of the enemy. This means that guerrillas, without a defended region of their own, must depend upon the people for their survival—not only to provide them food and support, but to spy upon the enemy.

Mao argued that guerrillas can exist for long periods in the enemy's rear, despite conventional wisdom to the contrary. Most people will support them and not betray them. This is especially true in rural areas and villages, where guerrillas are recruited from the local inhabitants and can merge into the population when they are not engaged in hostilities. The few traitors in such communities usually can be identified and eliminated. The people, Mao wrote, may be likened to water and the soldiers to the fish who inhabit it. "How may it be said that these two cannot exist together?"[8]

Mao said that guerrillas need bases for rest and training. In some places, especially mountainous regions, bases can be defended against enemy attack by following the methods Mao used in shielding his soviet in southeastern China against the KMT—that is, by ambushing isolated units and by attacking the supply lines and rear of the advancing enemy. But bases, important as they are, must be abandoned if the enemy surrounds the guerrillas and forces them into a defensive battle which they must win or die. Mao said: "The tactics of defense have no place in the realm of guerrilla warfare."

Mao recognized that, when the enemy successfully surrounds and attacks a base area, quick retreats expose protected villages in the area to enemy reprisals. This can mean not merely the destruction of the villages, but the killing or

8. Ibid., 93.

maiming of many of the people. Mao admitted it is difficult to explain retreats to villagers about to be abandoned. The only way to keep their support is to carry out fierce attacks on the logistic tail and other soft elements of the enemy—to show that the enemy is not getting off without loss.[9]

But Mao insisted that guerrillas cannot defend specific points or places. Guerrilla strength lies at the other extreme: the ability to strike fast and hard with small forces at vulnerable enemy targets, and then to get away. "The movements of guerrilla troops must be secret and of supernatural rapidity," Mao wrote. The enemy must be taken unaware and the guerrillas must move into action rapidly. "The basic method is the attack in a violent and deceptive form."[10]

In contrast, conventional armies are locked into static defense of their lines of communication and supply, bases, installations like airfields and ports, garrisons or outposts, and occupied cities. An orthodox army is especially vulnerable in its supply line. If it is broken, the invader's means of subsistence are lost. Therefore, the traditional army will go to any lengths to protect its supplies and depots. Strikes against these targets, even if they fail, will force the occupying power to divert a great part of its strength to guaranteeing delivery of food, ammunition, fuel, and other essential items.

Because the enemy is supersensitive to material factors, guerrillas can seize and retain the initiative—for they can select when, where, and how to attack vulnerable enemy points. The side that holds the initiative has liberty of action.

9. Nigel de Lee in Pimlott, 37.
10. Mao Zedong, 97.

The side that does not must respond to enemy moves, becoming passive and facing danger of defeat.

Guerrillas generally should operate in small units that act independently. In orthodox war, command must be centralized. In guerrilla war, Mao said, "this is not only undesirable but impossible."[11]

Mao emphasized that guerrillas must not allow the enemy to maneuver them into a position where they are robbed of initiative and where the decision to attack is forced on them. Even in defense, Mao said, all efforts must be directed toward resumption of the attack. It is only by attack that guerrillas can extinguish their enemy. A defense or a withdrawal is useless for destroying the enemy. The only value of either is to preserve troops.

If guerrilla forces get and keep the friendship of the people, they can call on them to provide vital information on enemy strength, plans, equipment, supply, and morale. In a guerrilla area, Mao wrote, every person can be an agent, including old men, women, boys, and girls.

With superior information, guerrillas can engage under conditions of their own choosing. Mao admonished guerrillas to fight only when chances of victory are heavily in their favor. When they do attack, they should make every effort to achieve maximum surprise and overwhelming superiority in numbers. They should strike at points where and when the enemy least expects them, and by ambush or by covert approach, at night, if possible. Attacks should be sudden, sharp, vicious, and of short duration.

Guerrillas should always withdraw rapidly after a suc-

11. Ibid., 52.

cessful attack, to avoid becoming the target for a counterstrike. They should almost never endure an attack. When an enemy strike comes, it should fall on empty air, the guerrillas already having vanished. Guerrillas also should withdraw before gaining a victory if the tide of battle abruptly turns against them. Nothing can be gained by remaining, because the enemy will almost always possess superior firepower and can cause heavy casualties quickly.

The basic tactic of guerrilla forces should be constant activity and movement. "There is nothing comparable to the fixed, passive defense that characterizes orthodox war," Mao wrote. And "there is in guerrilla warfare no such thing as a decisive battle."[12]

Since the training of most Western military leaders has emphasized the central significance of battle in winning wars, few have been able to comprehend the significance of this latter maxim of Mao's. A dramatic example of the almost polar-opposite thinking of traditional soldiers occurred after the Vietnam War. Colonel Harry G. Summers, Jr., an Army War College instructor and author of a book on military strategy, told a North Vietnamese colonel: "You never defeated us on the battlefield." To which his former enemy replied, "That may be so, but it is also irrelevant."[13]

Protracted war, which Mao Zedong's guerrilla strategy leads to, is the principal means that most weak powers today have to overcome aggression by a greater power. We will see in chapters 10–12 how the Vietnamese Communists used this theory to defeat both France and the United States—and how other powers might use it in the future.

12. Ibid., 52.
13. Karnow, 17.

Although Mao Zedong's theory on guerrilla warfare is considered by most scholars to be his contribution to the conduct of war, he and his military commanders showed in another war how a relatively weak China, using a different system, could neutralize the greatest military power on earth, the United States. This war, of course, was fought in Korea, from 1950 to 1953. In the next chapter, we will discuss Mao's second theory of warfare and what importance it has for the future.

NINE

Korea: Challenging the Strong Head to Head

WHEN THE CHINESE entered the Korean War in October 1950, their principal goal was to protect their historic Korean buffer. For most of a millennium Korea had served as a shield against incursions from Japan. After Japan's defeat, the United States became the danger from the sea.

The Chinese had nothing to do with dividing Korea along the 38th parallel in 1945 and the subsequent formation of a right-wing South Korea supported by the United States and a Communist North Korea supported by the Soviet Union. However, the arrangement suited China well, for North Korea became a buffer in front of the Chinese frontier along the Yalu River.

After U.S. commander Douglas MacArthur's invasion of Inchon in September 1950 led to the destruction of the North Korean army, the United States resolved to conquer the north and unite it with the south into a single U.S.-dominated state. The threat of an American army along the Yalu brought China into the war—and led to a very different strategy than Mao Zedong had employed in defeating the Nationalists.

For China it was imperative to keep the Americans off Chinese soil. Mao Zedong wanted to avoid the destruction inherent in such a clash, but the primary reason was to prevent the Nationalists in Taiwan from reentering the mainland as American allies. The administration of President Harry S. Truman had signaled its hostility to Red China from the outset and had formed an unofficial alliance with Chiang Kai-shek immediately after North Korea invaded the south on June 25, 1950.

China's overriding geopolitical imperative thus forced it to fight on the Korean peninsula. But the Chinese could not conduct a guerrilla war in Korea. Such a war, without a main line of resistance, would allow the Americans to advance directly into China. To ward off the possibility of invasion, Mao and Peng Dehuai, the Chinese commander in Korea, were obligated either to drive the Americans off the peninsula altogether, a virtually impossible task, or to establish a firm defensive line in Korea with regular troops manning it.

China was materially extremely weak compared to the United States. The Chinese possessed virtually no air force and few motorized vehicles, including trucks and tanks. Their armies were equipped with weapons from numerous sources, many obsolescent and some going back for three or four decades. Chinese industry in 1950 could manufacture rifles, machine guns, and mortars, with the ammunition for them, but could not build modern artillery pieces, jet aircraft, or other advanced weapons. The Chinese logistical system was primitive in the extreme. The Chinese brought some reserve stocks to forward railroad depots about thirty miles behind the front. But not much could be accomplished forward of the railheads because the Chinese relied for supplies on human and animal transport. Consequently, they fired mortars only on the most lucrative targets, and troops normally relied upon small arms, machine guns, and grenades.

The Chinese leaders recognized that they could not challenge American firepower directly. The methods they devised to emphasize their strengths and minimize their weaknesses demonstrate skills that other countries might use against us in the future.

The first job was to stop the United Nations advance, which was nearing the Yalu River.

Although extremely limiting in some respects, the Chinese dependence upon the backs of animals and soldiers liberated them from roads and permitted troops to fight anywhere they could walk, whether in front, on the side, or behind the enemy lines. UN forces, on the other hand, were tied to the roads because their supplies arrived by truck. The roads, therefore, were vulnerable to being cut by roadblocks.

During the Chinese civil war, Mao Zedong and his commanders had developed a highly effective method of dealing with more heavily armed Nationalist troops. Peng Dehuai now adapted these tactics to the Americans and their allies.

The Chinese tried whenever possible to infiltrate through enemy positions in order to plant a roadblock on the supply line, in hopes of inducing the enemy to retreat to regain contact with the rear. If UN forces stayed in position, the roadblocks still were useful in cutting off escape routes and supply.

In infiltration and assaults against front-line positions, the Chinese moved largely at night to avoid air strikes and reduce aerial observation. In attacks they tried to isolate individual outposts, usually platoons, by striking at the fronts, while at the same time attempting to outflank them. The purpose was to defeat forces in detail by gaining local superiority. If they could not destroy enemy positions, they hoped to induce the opponent to withdraw. When this failed, they got as close as possible to the enemy so that, when daylight came, U.S. aircraft would be unable to bomb them for fear of hitting friendly troops.

Advancing Chinese units generally followed the easiest, most accessible terrain in making their approaches: valleys, draws, or streambeds. As soon as they met resistance, they deployed, peeling off selected small units to engage the opposition. However, if they met no resistance, the whole column often moved in the darkness right past defensive emplacements deep into the rear of enemy positions. There were many examples of this in Korea. In some cases entire Chinese regiments marched in column formation into the UN rear.

Once fully committed, the Chinese seldom halted their attack, even when suffering heavy casualties. Other Chinese came forward to take the place of those killed or wounded. The buildup continued, often on several sides of the position, until they made a penetration—either by destroying the position or forcing the defenders to withdraw. After consolidating the new conquest, the Chinese then crept forward against the open flank of the next platoon position. This combination of stealth and boldness, usually executed in darkness against small units, could result in several penetrations of a battalion front and could be devastating.

Since the Chinese tried to cut the defending force into small fractions and attack these fractions with local superiority in numbers, they favored the ambush over all other tactical methods. As a rule attacking Chinese forces ranged in size from a platoon to a company (50 to 200 men) and were built up continually as casualties occurred.

The best defense was for the UN force somehow to hold its position until daybreak. With visibility restored, aircraft could attack the Chinese and usually restore the situation. However, Chinese night attacks were so effective that the counsel often went unheeded and defending forces were overrun or destroyed.[1]

On October 25, 1950, two South Korean infantry battalions ran into two separate Chinese roadblocks a few miles north of the Chongchon River, some fifty miles south of the Yalu.

The 3rd Battalion of the South Korean 6th Division's 2nd Regiment stopped eight miles northwest of Onjong when it came under Chinese fire. Shortly afterward, the Chinese threw another roadblock behind the battalion. The South Koreans panicked and about 350 died or were captured. Meanwhile the 2d Battalion arrived at Onjong, learned of the firefight ahead, moved out to rescue the 3d Battalion, but got only a few miles before it was halted also by Chinese roadblocks front and rear. The 2d Battalion escaped by moving across country back to Onjong, where the remainder of the regiment had taken up a defensive position. Only remnants of the 3d Battalion, all without weapons or vehicles, reached the village.

Korean anxiety mushroomed during the night. The Chinese with seeming ease had been able to walk through the

1. Alexander, Bevin, 300–03.

mountains on the Korean flanks, descend on the road behind, and establish blocks the Koreans could not break. At
3:30 A.M. on October 26 Chinese soldiers penetrated the Onjong position. The entire South Korean force immediately
abandoned the village and rushed back toward the Chongchon River. It got only three miles before striking still another Chinese roadblock. The South Koreans, completely
routed, abandoned their vehicles and weapons, scattered
into the hills, and made for the river as best they could.

A similar situation faced the 15th Regiment of the South
Korean 1st Division outside Unsan a few miles southwest of
Onjong. There a Chinese roadblock halted the regiment and
Chinese forces began slipping around its flanks. The regiment, though supported by American medium tanks, could
get nowhere. The division's 12th Regiment, following behind, turned west at Unsan and struck another Chinese roadblock just outside of town.

By daybreak on October 26 the Chinese had nearly surrounded Unsan, the two South Korean regiments having
retreated during the night. With the Koreans at Unsan were
two American tank companies and two artillery battalions.
Meanwhile the division's, third regiment, the 11th, had to
move south of Unsan because the Chinese had cut the main
supply route in an envelopment from the west.

The 11th Regiment cleared the main supply road, but the
other two regiments made only slight gains. The Koreans
found the Chinese to be exceptionally well camouflaged and
dug-in, and extremely hard to locate. Aided by heavy artillery
concentrations from American guns and repeated strafing
runs by American aircraft, the Koreans attacked over the next
three days, but could make no gains against Chinese troops
using only mortars, automatic weapons, and small arms.

On November 1, 1950, the American commander, Lieutenant General Walton H. Walker, sent in the U.S. 8th Cavalry Regiment (really an infantry outfit) to relieve the battered 11th and 12th South Korean Regiments. But over the next two days, the Chinese forced the 8th Cavalry's 1st and 2d Battalions into precipitate retreat and surrounded and virtually destroyed the 3d Battalion.

The Chinese then drew off, probably hopeful that the Americans would heed their warning blow and stop their rush to the Yalu. However, Douglas MacArthur insisted on continuing the offensive, and, on November 24, 1950, sent his forces forward. The Chinese repeated their tactics of infiltration and roadblocks front and rear and forced the entire UN army into headlong flight. Nearly a third of the U.S. 2d Division was destroyed and large elements of the U.S. 1st Marine Division and the army 7th Division were surrounded and destroyed at Changjin (Chosin) Reservoir, and the survivors were forced to undergo a terrible retreat to the sea under incredibly difficult winter conditions.

The Chinese tried to push the Americans far back into South Korea but did not have the strength to drive them out. Not only were Chinese weapons decidedly inferior, but China could not mount a sustained offensive since the Americans had overwhelming superiority in the air and U.S. aircraft could interdict most supplies coming by road and railway. Since Chinese attacks had to be conducted with supplies brought forward secretly, at night, and carried mostly on the backs of porters and animals, Chinese offensives always petered out after advances of fifty or sixty miles—when the Chinese soldiers ran out of supplies.[2]

2. The Americans retreated about 120 miles from near the Yalu to about the Thirty-eighth parallel after the first Chinese offensive in November—

The Chinese offensives also were costly because American air power and artillery exacted heavy casualties on troops having to advance in the open. As a result, the Chinese command decided, after its May 1951 drive failed, to abandon offensive war entirely and move over to the defense.

The Chinese probably all along had planned a shift to the defense if they could not induce the United States to withdraw from the peninsula. China's defensive strategy—which continued until the armistice more than two years later—demonstrated that Mao and his generals had found another method than guerrilla warfare to stalemate a much more powerful enemy. The same method can be used today, but the expense of it is tremendous.

The Chinese realized they had to establish a battle line, but to do so they had to neutralize American artillery and air-dropped bombs and napalm.

The Chinese did not have an air force capable of challenging American air supremacy and their relatively few artillery pieces mostly remained far in the rear because American command of the sky prevented bringing up enough shells to make them effective. The Chinese consequently continued to rely on rifles, machine guns, mortars, and hand grenades.

The only way the Chinese could both maintain a battle line and keep their troops from being destroyed was to burrow into the ground. The result was a continuous line across the waist of Korea consisting of deep bunkers dug into Korean mountainsides, roofed with thick timbers over which were placed heavy piles of rocks or earth.

United States military leaders were stunned by the rapid materialization of this bristling main line of resistance. But

December 1950. However, this withdrawal was not primarily due to Chinese pressure but rather because American morale was shattered by the surprise Chinese offensive.

they and political leaders back home were so angry with China for having foiled their original effort to seize the north that they inaugurated a series of attacks on this line in the late summer and early fall of 1951. They ordered the assaults despite the fact that they had privately, though not publicly, renounced efforts to conquer North Korea. Thus the battles had no strategic purpose whatsoever.

Employing immense artillery bombardments and aerial strikes with bombs and napalm, the Americans attempted to knock out the enemy bunkers at the points on the Communist line they planned to assault. The preliminary bombardments and strikes went on for days. In the cases of the most intense of these efforts, against Bloody Ridge and Heartbreak Ridge in eastern Korea, shellfire and bombs destroyed all vegetation and left the hills as cratered and barren as a moonscape.

American commanders hoped that the shelling and bombs would eliminate most of the bunkers and enemy so the infantry could just walk up the ridgelines and occupy the heights with few losses. They found, however, that bombs and shells destroyed only a few of the bunkers. The Chinese and North Korean soldiers waited out the infernos deep in the ground. When the bombs and shelling stopped, they pulled out their weapons and directed highly accurate fire and rolled grenades down the slopes onto the UN infantry as it climbed the fingers leading to the ridgetops.

The result was a series of inconceivably bloody firefights that cost both sides huge losses. American and other UN troops suffered relatively less because of their massive firepower. But the total effect was staggering: an estimated 234,000 Communist and 60,000 UN casualties, most of them American, during the period of the battles on the ridge lines from August to November 1951, when they ceased.

The only gains by American and UN forces were a few shattered hillsides. Their capture not only did not change the strategic situation in Korea, but they scarcely affected the tactical situation either. For behind every hill the UN captured rose another hill, also covered with Communist bunkers. To seize that hill would have required another stupendous effort. And behind the second hill rose still another hill which could have been armored with bunkers.

The American commanders at last decided that the cost of assaults against the ridge lines was too great and they called them off. The Chinese could sustain high casualties far longer than the Americans could. China was an authoritarian state and controlled all of the media; thus the extent of Chinese losses was not generally known to the Chinese people. This was *not* the case for the American people, who did know of the United States' losses. The war entered into a stalemate that was not broken until the armistice in July 1953.

The United States could have ended this deadlock only by an amphibious landing around one of the flanks. This would have required an immense effort. And, since it could not have been concealed entirely, the Chinese could have prepared a fierce resistance.

China's experience in Korea demonstrates how extremely difficult a defensive strategy is for a weaker power to carry out. It indicates that such a strategy can be sustained only by a country with immense manpower resources and a political system that permits it to hide its price from the people.

China's losses in killed and wounded in Korea were

about 900,000 men, the overwhelming bulk of them suffered in the defensive phase of the war. Total American casualties were about 140,000, but 28,000 of these came before China entered.[3]

This enormous disparity—eight times as many losses for China as for the United States—is a reflection of the tremendous superiority of firepower that the United States could bring to bear and how effective this firepower can be when directed against known concentrations of enemy troops, however well shielded by fortifications. In a guerrilla war firepower largely is wasted, because the quarry usually has flown before gunships, bombers, and artillery are brought to bear. *Life* magazine calculated in 1967 that it cost the United States $400,000 to kill a single Vietcong guerrilla. The cost included 75 bombs and 150 artillery shells.[4]

Therefore, one of the salient advantages of guerrilla over positional warfare is that guerrillas largely neutralize the greatest strength, firepower, of the enemy and force him to engage on terms more nearly equal. In Korea the Chinese developed a method to reduce, but not to eliminate wholly, the effect of American firepower. This reduction permitted China to turn the Korean War into a standoff, but at a staggering cost.

And the Chinese were compelled to use colossal numbers of troops, well over half a million at any one time, in manning their line across Korea. The expense would have been even greater except for the fact that the waist of Korea is fairly narrow, about 120 miles. This made it feasible to construct a front that was not impossibly long.

3. Alexander, Bevin, 483.
4. Bilton and Sim, 33.

The greatest disadvantage today in a strategy such as the one that China followed in Korea remains in challenging American firepower directly. Where U.S. forces have identifiable targets and can bring their weapons to bear, their capability for destruction is awesome. Bunker-type defenses are less effective today because accuracy and deadliness of weapons have increased greatly in the past four decades. Although enterprising forces can still hide positions from the enemy, American detection systems could find and weapons could destroy a much higher percentage of emplacements than they were able to do in the Korean War.

Consequently, the argument against most powers challenging American military power directly remains compelling. China or another large nation with much manpower might duplicate the Korean War solution with defensive positions of great strength in the hope of deflecting American missiles and bombs. Such a strategy might prevent American occupation of the country or large parts of it, and might be justifiable in some cases. A manpower-rich country also might elect to occupy part of a neighbor's territory and then shift over to a defensive line, creating a Korea-like stalemate. However, a defensive approach would be essentially a fortress strategy, and the defending power would have to abandon offensive war and the benefits of a decisive solution that an offensive might bring. It would have to wait until the United States became weary and withdrew. Also, the expense to the defending nation in lives and property would be gigantic.

These are the reasons why Mao Zedong's guerrilla warfare strategy—which leaves the initiative in the hands of the invaded country—holds the most promise for most countries confronting American power.

TEN

Giap: Neutralizing Military Power

FROM THE POINT OF VIEW of lessons for the future, our most instructive adversaries have been the Communists in the Vietnam War.

Using the theory of protracted war developed by Mao Zedong, the North Vietnamese and Vietcong attacked us at our weakest positions. By refusing to defend battle positions—except during two short periods—and by striking anywhere in the country, usually with small forces, they obligated the United States to disperse its power widely and to employ large numbers of troops to defend American bases against assault while reserving other forces to search for and destroy the enemy.

The process reduced the conflict to a war of attrition, which exacted a steady penalty of American killed and wounded, but offered no foreseeable end. This ultimately turned the American people against the war, and forced the United States to withdraw.

The struggle in Vietnam demonstrated how a sophisticated but weak opponent can confront and counter American military technology and power. The lesson can be applied by almost any country invaded by a foreign power.

The Americans considered the Communists in South Vietnam to be insurgents seeking to overthrow the South Vietnamese government. Consequently, our leaders talked about conducting "counterinsurgent" warfare. The Communists, on the other hand, felt they represented the nationalist aspirations of the Vietnamese people, North and South, and maintained the Saigon government of South Vietnam was a puppet regime, propped up by the imperialist United States. Although the United States held it was protecting an ally (and keeping southeast Asia from falling like dominos to the Kremlin), to the Vietnamese Communists the United States was an invading power.

The United States could repeat this scenario by aiding one side in an internal conflict. It also could invade another country and act more openly as an aggressor. In either case, the methods used by the Vietcong and North Vietnamese can be followed by forces unable to stand up directly to American military power. A unified and resolute country is more capable of succeeding with the Vietcong strategy than a country, like South Vietnam, which harbored internal divisions. The United States must have overwhelming reasons for deploying forces in a hostile land, because the likelihood is great that its forces will become bogged down in a protracted war with steady losses and no resolution.

The Communist leaders in Hanoi learned how to defeat the United States by winning an earlier war against France. As we saw in chapter 8, they got their strategy from Mao Zedong, who developed a method for weak forces to overcome strong as a result of Communist-Nationalist clashes in China in the late 1920s and early 1930s. Mao inherited his principles from the father of Chinese military strategy, Sun Tzu, who wrote his classic volume on the art of war about 400 B.C.

Sun Tzu was unknown in the West until modern times. But a number of Western thinkers developed many of his principles independently. One of them—building walls around cities—was an effective means for a weaker side to deter conquest by a stronger until the development of siege cannon. Moreover, walls symbolize a strategy that does not challenge the enemy's strength but exploits his weakness. That is, the power of ancient aggressors lay in armor, blades, spears, and arrows, but these were of small use in breaking stones and masonry or scaling high walls made of them.

Consequently, the sources of the Vietnamese victory over the United States lie deep in the theory of warfare. They have little to do with technology and superior weapons, the current American strong suit. Instead, they rest on concepts or ideas of surprise, deception, avoiding what is strong, and attacking what is weak.

When Japan surrendered to the Allies in August 1945, the Communist and nationalist leader, Ho Chi Minh, declared Vietnam independent from its colonial overlord, France, which had ruled it and neighboring Cambodia and Laos as French Indochina since late in the nineteenth century. France refused to accept the loss of its imperial position and embarked on a war with the insurgents, who took the name Vietminh (or national independence movement).

The Vietminh possessed a great general in Vo Nguyen Giap (born 1912), who adapted the teachings of Sun Tzu and Mao Zedong to the conditions he faced against the French. The solutions he reached were so effective that, by May 1954, he had forced a French army to surrender at Dien Bien Phu in northwestern Vietnam and so shattered French confidence that Paris abandoned Indochina at the Geneva conference immediately following.

The essence of Giap's success was to attack the French indirectly, avoiding their firepower, which was many times what the Vietminh could bring to bear. Giap employed virtually the same system against the Americans when they intervened in 1965, successfully adjusting to the even greater U.S. firepower and mobility, especially by helicopter-borne troops who could alight at almost any point they chose. The principles Giap employed are valid today.

Giap summarized his theory of indirect war as follows: "Is the enemy strong? One avoids him. Is he weak? One attacks him. To his modern equipment, one opposes a boundless heroism to vanquish either by harassing or by combining military operations with political and economic action; there is no fixed line of demarcation, the front being wherever the enemy is found." Giap called for concentrating troops to achieve overwhelming superiority at a point where the enemy is exposed, with the aim of destruction of the enemy force. Although his forces might be inferior overall, they could achieve absolute superiority "in a given place, and at a given time." Giap urged his men to exhaust the enemy by small victories. The main objective, he insisted, is to destroy enemy manpower. To achieve this, he stressed the tactical principles of "initiative, flexibility, rapidity, surprise, suddenness in attack and retreat."[1]

Giap's method rested on accurate, up-to-date intelligence of French actions and intentions, detailed planning of each

1. Giap, 105.

operation, and his tactical principles, the most important of which were speed of movement and surprise.[2]

The Vietminh emphasized speed in all phases of combat. Giap trained his soldiers to concentrate quickly, take battle positions at once, and not linger in one area, where they might be spotted and attacked. The usual pattern was to form up a Vietminh force some distance from the objective, to march secretly two or three nights, and to attack, getting maximum surprise. In case of retreat, speed also was vital. Giap emphasized that a Vietminh force should never be caught without a way to retreat. This might be a specific route from the battle area or a plan for soldiers to "melt" into the population and "disappear."

Surprise, combined with speed, secrecy, and deception, was essential to Vietminh success. The usual technique was to arouse French suspicions at one or more false attack points, but to strike at a wholly unexpected place. To delude the French, the Vietminh leaked misleading information to double agents, and marched forces in the direction of a pretended target to give the impression of large troop movements, then moved stealthily at night in the real direction of attack, avoiding villages and inhabited areas to reduce chances of being detected. As a general rule, the Vietminh struck only if they had many more troops than the enemy guarding an objective. But they believed that, with the right combination of surprise and deception, a small Vietminh unit could often overwhelm a larger.

The Vietminh depended almost entirely upon small infantry units. Some were organized as guerrilla detachments, others as regular military forces. Although these regulars

2. The summary of Vietminh tactical principles is largely drawn from Tanham, 74–77, 83–96.

were formed into battalions, regiments, and ultimately divisions, the emphasis was on operations by company-sized or
smaller units (under 200 men).[3] Occasionally small detachments would combine for a larger operation, but frequently
they struck at objectives on their own. This meant that almost any French or puppet installation anywhere in Vietnam
might be attacked at any time, forcing the French to disperse
their forces and creating a deep sense of insecurity.

The Vietminh relied primarily on infantry weapons,
some of which were old or obsolescent. Later, they received
modern weapons from China and the Soviet Union, but
they possessed no aircraft and no armored vehicles and used
artillery in significant amounts only in the last months of the
war. Instead, they employed rifles, machine guns, recoilless
rifles, mortars, hand grenades, and satchel charges of explo-

3. Giap formed three types of forces: the regular army, regional forces,
and popular troops. Until the first divisions were created in 1950, the
largest regular forces were regiments. Divisions originally had 15,000 men
but by 1953 were down to about 9,500. There were three infantry regiments
in each division, plus artillery and heavy mortar detachments, and engineer, headquarters, and support troops. Independent regiments remained
important, however. Their largest weapons were usually recoilless rifles
and mortars. Regional forces were organized on a territorial basis (much
as were the commandos of the Afrikaners in the Boer War of 1899–1902).
Each province normally had a battalion of regional troops, made up of
companies organized in each of the province's local districts. Popular or
irregular forces were formed at the village level and consisted of two
groups: *Dan Quan*, of both sexes and all ages, with auxiliary duties, and
Dan Quan du Kich, men aged 18–45, who served as part-time guerrillas,
and operated in groups of eight to fifteen men. Regular forces were the
Vietminh elite. They were the most highly trained and equipped and
normally were engaged in combat only when victory was certain. Regional
troops were less well organized, trained, and equipped. Their primary
duty was to protect their area and its population. Of the popular forces,
only the *du Kich* undertook guerrilla operations, generally on a small scale.
Since they were part-time soldiers, they got less training and generally
were forbidden to assemble in large groups. The *Dan Quan* primarily
made up a labor force. See Tanham, 33–52.

sives. These weapons could be carried on the backs of soldiers or by bearers and freed the Vietminh from reliance on heavy service units or a protected supply line. This was the reverse of the French, who followed Western military doctrine in emphasizing heavy weapons, tanks, and combat aircraft. This equipment required immense amounts of fuel and ammunition and forced the French to rely on a huge logistics train, trucks, and highways, and obligated them to defend their bases in order to stay alive.

The light logistics burden freed the Vietminh infantry from dependence on bases and gave them great mobility. They were not bound to the roads, could march across country and along jungle paths, could infiltrate almost anywhere, hide from air observation and attacks, and emerge wherever they chose. Mobility made the Vietminh doctrine of surprise much easier to carry out.

Mobility was the key to nearly all Vietminh operations. Giap ordered his forces, in most cases, to accept battle only under conditions that favored a quick victory. Their instructions were to slip away when in danger of attack from superior forces. Although the doctrine was hit-and-run, Vietminh guerrilla detachments had a different function than Vietminh regular forces. The aim of guerrillas was to cause confusion, destroy property, and keep the enemy anxious and off balance. The aim of the regular forces was annihilation of an enemy post or detachment—and regulars were normally committed only when there was likelihood of such total destruction.

The Vietminh accepted Mao Zedong's axiom that offensive warfare is the only way to defeat or discourage the enemy. Consequently, they renounced the defensive. Giap also followed the doctrine of Mao that guerrilla warfare alone will never insure defeat of the enemy. He saw guerrilla war as a phase to wear down the resistance and the will of the French. When the French were sufficiently weakened and their resolve diminished, the Vietminh had to move to conventional war, confront the French army head-to-head, and defeat it.[4]

Until this was achieved, the Vietminh remained in the guerrilla phase. But this phase was almost entirely offensive. To insure successful attacks, the Vietminh made careful plans and preparations and tried to launch their assaults at times when the enemy least expected them or when they were least able to respond. They spied on garrisons to discover weaknesses or habits that might be exploited. For example, they sought to locate guards who customarily were not alert, and tried to plan their attacks when these guards were on duty. In the attack, each unit got a specific job and officers instructed the members of the unit in detail as to what was required and what the leadership hoped to achieve. In this way, the common soldiers became active participants and enthusiastic supporters.

The Vietminh generally approached a French position by infiltration at night. They developed great skill in this and often departed the battlefield by this method as well. Infiltration implied a stealthy approach, usually with soldiers moving individually and at wide intervals. The technique concealed the approaching Communists from air attack, and normally from ground detection. It also unnerved French

4. Mao Zedong postulated three phases in protracted war. Phase 1: agitation and getting the support of the masses. Phase 2: guerrilla operations and establishing bases. Phase 3: open warfare to topple the government. Hence moving to conventional warfare is often referred to by writers as "phase 3," while guerrilla warfare is "phase 2." See Krepinevich, 7.

forces, for Vietminh units sometimes infiltrated right through enemy positions, enabling them to attack the position on two sides.

The aim was complete surprise. To this end, the Vietminh generally dispensed with preparatory fires and assaulted around midnight or shortly thereafter. The Vietminh considered the French poor night fighters. Part of the reason for this perception was that the French customarily clung to their vehicles, making it hard for them to fight in the bush at night. Also, enemy aircraft and artillery could not find Vietminh forces as well as in daylight. The Communists tried to achieve a breakthrough on a very narrow front, sometimes committing nine-tenths of the attack force to the main assault, leaving the remainder to make noisy, diversionary attacks and demonstrations.

Well outside the enemy perimeter, the Vietminh usually set up a heavy weapons group, normally of machine guns, mortars and recoilless rifles, with the task of destroying at the outset one or two important enemy positions (like the radio, command post or heavy weapons). The hope was to distract and demoralize the defenders by making them feel isolated and vulnerable.

The actual attack normally opened with a small engineer or sapper force which infiltrated to a critical point and tried to blow a breach with dynamite, sometimes tied on the end of a bamboo pole so it could be inserted into wire entanglements. Following behind were assault infantry units, which attempted to rush in and overwhelm the French post. In reserve was another force with the mission of covering the shock troops with fire, assisting them in the attack, if successful, or covering their retreat, if repulsed.

Giap emphasized that attacking troops should penetrate

as deeply as possible into the enemy position and not allow themselves to be stopped at the periphery, where French defensive weapons could normally stop them and inflict heavy casualties.

Three other rules were: (1) when the enemy attacked frontally, the Vietminh were to counterattack, not directly against the French main effort, but at another, weak, point; (2) when caught in an artillery barrage, the Communists were either to retreat, dig in and wait for their own artillery or mortar support, or, if close, to "cling" to the enemy, so his artillery would be unable to strike without fear of hitting his own forces as well; (3) when cut off or encircled, troops were either to concentrate and break through at one point, or disband, and allow each man to seek his own way out.

Because the French possessed insufficient transport aircraft to supply their many posts by air, they relied on roads to move troops and deliver food, ammunition and other goods. The Vietminh, therefore, possessed ready-made opportunities for ambush and for cutting communications. The Communists attempted to deny use of the roads to the French by mining them, destroying bridges, or by mounting roadblocks and attacks. Small parties of guerrillas or regional troops set up traps for isolated French vehicles or units, while Vietminh regulars staged major ambushes against larger formations, especially relief forces. Indeed, the Communists often generated their own ambushes by besieging a French or loyalist outpost, making no serious effort to capture it, but inducing the French to send a rescue expedition from the nearest base. The Vietminh, knowing the route along which the relief force would move, were able to set up an ambush at the most advantageous position.

The Communists developed an orderly system of traps.

One element, often a company, set up positions, usually on elevations on both sides of the road, to halt the head of the column. About 500 to 1,000 yards farther back on the road they hid the main attack force, four or five times the size of the lead element, while in the rear they posted a third element to close off the end of the column and keep it from retreating.

The main attack force and the rear roadblock force allowed the column to proceed past unhindered, and only burst onto the sides and rear of the French with intense fire after the head of the convoy had been stopped. Because of excellent Vietminh camouflage, the French almost never could detect ambushes, even when aircraft flew over the route searching for enemy forces. They made the convoys more defensible by carrying along armor or artillery, but never were able to prevent the attacks. The French feared ambushes to the end of the war.

The Vietminh avoided defensive combat whenever possible. This meant they did not defend positions. They thus conducted a strategy that was the opposite that of the French, who were obligated to hold positions—cities, supply bases, forts, and communication routes. This was the only way the French could remain in Vietnam.

The Vietminh gained their strength from the people. They devoted immense efforts to enlist or induce loyalty, promising to give the peasants land and to reduce their taxes, interest on loans and forced labor, and assassinating leaders who opposed them. On the whole, the populace also supported the Vietminh because they were attempting to oust imperialist France and to gain independence. The native backers of the French constituted a small minority who benefited economically and socially from French rule, notably officials, professional people, and landlords who rented out farmland and made loans to peasants.

The Vietminh did possess a few bases where their troops could rest and be trained, and where supplies could be stored. But these bases were in difficult, remote, usually mountainous regions beyond the reach of French ground forces. The most important were in Viet Bac along the Chinese frontier, a jungle-clad, mountainous, cave-honey-combed region, often obscured from the air by mists. The French tried to evict the Vietminh in 1947, but failed.

However, the Vietminh were prepared to abandon any base rather than be drawn into battle to hold it. Their reasoning was that the French, with vastly greater firepower and possessing complete command of the air, could always win a stand-up fight, and inflict terrible casualties in the process. To defend a point would be to play into the hands of the enemy. Consequently, the Vietminh possessed plans to retreat at any time from any position.

For example, in August 1948, the French discovered the headquarters of the Vietminh commander in a swampy area of the Mekong River delta in southern Vietnam. While several battalions moved rapidly overland toward the post, two companies of paratroopers descended directly on the command post. The Vietminh defended fiercely for a few moments, but, at a given signal, broke contact and disappeared. The French could not find them.

The Vietminh had two means of disappearing. One was to retreat into previously prepared hiding places—caves, holes, tunnels, and positions along riverbanks with entry below the water level. The other was to retreat in small groups or individually. The soldiers fled into the woods or jungles or melted into the population of a neighboring village or city.

The Communists would not hold villages, even those whose people were committed to their cause. But they often made attacks on villages painful and costly to the French and their puppet soldiers. A network of guards—often peasants, male or female, adults or children—patrolled access points to a given village and quickly got word of the approach of an enemy force. The Vietminh frequently tried to entice the French into prepared traps or ambushes. Sometimes this worked, sometimes it did not. When a French force small enough to be annihilated approached, the Vietminh tried to draw it into the village, where they could counterattack and hopefully destroy it. If the force was too large and well-armed, the Vietminh did not engage in a hopeless defense, but disengaged and disappeared.

General Giap always sought to move from guerrilla warfare, which merely weakened and demoralized the French, into open, conventional war using regular forces that could challenge the enemy directly and defeat him. Giap made the mistake of moving to this final stage prematurely in the spring of 1951 in the Red River delta of northern Vietnam. Against heavy French bombing and artillery concentrations, the Communist regulars suffered a resounding defeat, leaving many thousands of dead and wounded.

Giap wisely returned to the guerrilla phase and sought ways to force the French to disperse their forces even farther. He concluded that the French were determined to keep control of Laos and could be lured into reinforcing garrisons there if the Vietminh threatened it. In the fall of 1952 he sent three divisions in the direction of Laos and in April 1953 came within a few miles of the Laotian capital, Luang Prabang, before withdrawing to avoid the upcoming rainy season.

The new French commander, General Henri Navarre, adopted a new plan which he believed would regain the initiative. The idea was to establish a "mooring point" *(mole d'amarrage)*, a fortified base from which the French could penetrate into Vietminh rear areas. Navarre established a mooring point at Dien Bien Phu, a narrow valley five miles wide and eleven long near the Laotian border in northwestern Vietnam. At Dien Bien Phu, Navarre believed, French forces could protect Laos from the Vietminh.[5]

French air force leaders protested the move because Dien Bien Phu had extremely poor road communications with the rest of Vietnam and was 200 air miles west of principal French air bases around Hanoi. If Dien Bein Phu had to be supplied by air, the effort would greatly overtax French transport capacity. Navarre, however, was confident Giap could not respond in strength and sent in a force of French paratroops to occupy Dien Bien Phu in the fall of 1953.

Giap now saw an opportunity to move into open warfare with the French. Although the 13,000 troops Navarre finally put into Dien Bien Phu represented only about 5 percent of total French power in Indochina, Giap and the Communist leadership believed a resounding defeat there could induce the French people to abandon the war. Giap saw that the French were in an isolated position and, if road connections could be cut, would be dependent on airlifted supplies. Here was a chance for annihilation.

Giap moved 50,000 troops toward Dien Bien Phu, with

5. Karnow, 189–98.

20,000 more along the communications line. He cut road communications, but his most important decision was to bring in ninety-six 75- or 105-millimeter artillery howitzers, and a number of 120mm heavy mortars, which his men laboriously pulled on top of the hills surrounding the base. Getting these guns, plus ammunition for them, across the atrocious roads and paths of northwestern Vietnam was a herculean task, requiring thousands of porters. But the guns gave Giap a decisive advantage. He was certain they could overwhelm the twenty-eight artillery pieces the French had emplaced. With their artillery gone, the French would be unable to respond or to escape, and dependent on airlifted supplies. To reduce air flights, Giap also assembled eighty 37mm and a hundred 20mm antiaircraft guns, plus a number of .50-caliber machine guns with antiaircraft mounts.[6]

The French had anticipated using tanks to defend Dien Bien Phu, but thick bush entangled the armor and made it unable to reach the Vietminh artillery on the hills. These guns now pounded the valley, destroying most of the French artillery, and dropping shells on the airstrip. French fighter-bombers tried to locate and destroy the guns but the Vietminh expertly camouflaged them while antiaircraft guns destroyed many of the French aircraft—as well as transports attempting to bring in supplies. The French were reduced to parachuting in supplies, a large quantity of which fell into Vietminh lines.

Navarre had expected a headlong assault. But Giap knew his men were inexperienced in attacking fortified, entrenched French positions and, instead, besieged Dien Bien Phu, creeping closer and closer to the French by means of tunnels

6. Klonis, 130–32.

and trenches, gradually encircling the base with a network several hundred miles long.

Giap wrote after the battle: "The greatest surprise we had in store for the enemy was our refusal to engage in all-out lightning clashes with the elite entire strength of the [French] Expeditionary Corps, firmly dug in their solidly built forts. We decided to destroy pockets of resistance one by one, and gradually, in our own way, at a time and place of our own choosing, launch attacks with overwhelming superiority in each battle and at the same time consolidate our bunker system and cut the enemy's supply line until the base camp was strangled."[7]

On May 7, 1954, the Vietminh red flag went up over Dien Bien Phu as the last French holdouts surrendered. The next day delegates assembled at Geneva for a peace conference. France, defeated and demoralized, surrendered Indochina and withdrew. Ho Chi Minh and Giap had won their first war of liberation. But another was to follow with the United States.

7. George Esper, Associated Press, Roanoke (Va.) *Times and World-News*, B1, May 1, 1994.

ELEVEN

Why the Vietnam War
Was a Mistake

A T THE GENEVA CONFERENCE China and the Soviet
Union forced Ho Chi Minh to accept a "temporary" division
of Vietnam at the 17th parallel pending an all-Vietnam election, to be held in two years. The Soviet Union acted to keep
France from joining the European Defense Community and
a supranational European army. China wanted peace to prevent an American presence on its southern frontier.

The conference thus produced North Vietnam, ruled
from Hanoi by the Communists, and South Vietnam, which
immediately came under the tutelage of the United States.
The right-wing government in Saigon and its American
sponsors had no intention of allowing a nationwide election
because they knew the Communists would win it.

The titular Vietnamese emperor, Bao Dai, more interested in revelries along the French Riviera than rebuilding
his nation, appointed Ngo Dinh Diem, a Roman Catholic
bachelor, as prime minister of South Vietnam. Diem created
a narrow, authoritative oligarchy composed principally of

his own family and Catholic cronies. The oligarchy exploited
its offices for personal gain, persecuted Buddhists, and opposed reform, protecting the holdings of large landlords and
requiring peasants to pay for land given to them by the
Vietminh.

Diem purged all the Vietminh he could find. These killings, plus his refusal to hold an all-Vietnam election, finally
set off a new revolt. The insurgents, now called the Vietcong
or VC, were directed from Hanoi. In May 1959 Hanoi en-
larged the Ho Chi Minh Trail through Laos and Cambodia,
which the Vietminh had used to infiltrate men and weapons
into the south, and began to organize resistance and to assas-
sinate officials of the Saigon government.

Intense popular opposition to Diem, led by Buddhists,
threatened to set off a non-Communist revolt in South Vietnam. Meanwhile, the South Vietnamese army—despite immense material aid in weapons and training by the United
States—was unable to challenge the Vietcong in battle.
These twin dangers induced the United States to encourage
a coup by South Vietnamese generals in November 1963. The
result was the assassination of Diem and his corrupt brother,
Nhu, and the installation of the first of a series of military
regimes, which represented no popular forces and depended
entirely on American support.

American leaders intervened because they were determined to "save" South Vietnam. If it went Communist, so
went the "falling-domino theory," the rest of southeast Asia
would fall to the Kremlin. This was nonsense, as proved by
the eagerness of the Soviet Union and China to sell out Ho
Chi Minh at the Geneva convention. But U.S. leaders refused to believe the evidence and allowed the United States
to be drawn inexorably into Vietnam.

The Vietcong were generally locally recruited guerrillas, corresponding to regional and popular forces under the old Vietminh organization. North Vietnamese troops, soon introduced, were members of regular army units and represented the best trained, best equipped forces the Communists possessed. But they were much inferior in firepower to the South Vietnamese army, and still possessed no air force, whereas Saigon had many American-supplied aircraft, including both transport and attack helicopters, which added a new dimension of mobility and lethality.

However, the South Vietnamese army reflected the corruption that permeated the government. It was unable to defeat the Communists because it was structured to uphold the regime, not fight guerrillas. Promotion in the South Vietnamese army depended upon loyalty to Diem or, later, to the current military coup leader. Competence or resolve to defeat the Communists played little role in selecting commanders. Also, venality led many officers and soldiers to exploit the peasants and other people rather than fight the Communists.

Consequently, the North Vietnamese and the Vietcong were able to conduct a highly effective guerrilla war, using the same strategy and tactics worked out against the French by Vo Nguyen Giap.

The inability of the Saigon army to counter the Communists convinced President Lyndon B. Johnson that American forces had to take over conduct of the war. But U.S. leaders did not understand that the key to defeating the Vietcong was not battle at all. It was removing the abuses of power by the elites and ending the exploitation of the common people, thereby undermining their support of the Communists. The struggle was political, not military. The purpose of armies is to fight war. In war one side tries to end the armed resistance of the other. It is not a process for reaching mutual agreement on social, economic, and political change. War may bring about the conditions by which change can occur, but war itself is an act of violence, of force, of compulsion.

American leaders were wrong in committing an army to solve a political problem. Yet they persisted in believing that the Communists could be defeated on the battlefield. They seized on any evidence of combat success as proof. However, American military leaders were frustrated by the elusiveness of such success, a frustration crystallized by Lieutenant Colonel John Paul Vann and other American advisers who insisted the Vietcong could be whipped "if they would only stand and fight."[1]

The American military was further confused by its preoccupation with fighting a "mid-intensity" war against the Soviet Union. Mid-intensity war was a step below "high-intensity" (nuclear war), and emphasized heavy weapons, direct confrontation of the enemy, set-piece battles, high expenditures of ammunition, bombs, and missiles, and occupation of enemy territory. Military leaders found it difficult to understand the "low-intensity conflict" (LIC) being waged by the Communists in Vietnam, which depended upon lightly armed infantry, firepower restraint, and was wholly unconcerned with holding ground.

President John F. Kennedy wanted the army to be capable of "flexible response," able to fight both a mid-intensity war and an LIC. In a speech to the graduating class at West Point in 1962, he demonstrated his understanding of how different an LIC is: "This is another type of war, new in its

1. Karnow, 259–62.

intensity, ancient in its origins, war by guerrillas, subversion, insurgents, assassins; war by ambush instead of by combat; by infiltration, instead of aggression; seeking victory by evading and exhausting the enemy instead of engaging him. . . . It requires . . . a whole new kind of strategy, a wholly different kind of force."[2]

President Kennedy saw correctly that the Communists were conducting a war far different from the one the Pentagon was planning to fight. But he concluded that American military forces could challenge insurgents directly and defeat them, when the only way to defeat insurgency is to remove the baneful economic and social conditions which caused revolt in the first place.

In any event, the U.S. Army remained oriented to midintensity conflict in Europe and carried this concept into Vietnam. Confusion as to the nature of low-intensity conflicts, as well as confidence in American firepower, led military leaders to view their task in Vietnam as almost identical to the potential conflict in Europe against the Soviet Union.

This led them to decide, for example, that an abject South Vietnamese defeat in January 1963 was a victory because the Vietcong had retreated after the battle. Since the Saigon forces "remained in possession of the battlefield" and occupied enemy territory, so the theory ran, they had won. This exhibited a thorough misunderstanding of the nature of guerrilla war.

The government forces-Vietcong clash occurred at Ap Bac, a village in the Mekong delta forty miles southwest of Saigon. Its conduct and outcome illustrate both the success-

2. Krepinevich, 30.

ful tactics of the Communists and the incompetence of the South Vietnamese leadership. A South Vietnamese force cornered a Vietcong unit only one-tenth its size and infinitely inferior in weapons. The government troops planned a three-pronged pincer—a regiment landing by helicopter on the north, two battalions approaching by foot from the south, and a squadron aboard armored personnel carriers (APCs) moving from the west.

The VC were emplaced along a canal with a clear line of fire across rice paddies. They held their fire as three waves of choppers landed most of the infantry regiment. As the fourth wave arrived, the guerrillas opened up with automatic-weapons fire, downing five helicopters. Three American crew members died and the South Vietnamese regiment made no advance. The armor commander deployed his APCs slowly and individually so they became easy targets, and the armored assault fizzled. The commander of the two battalions supposed to advance from the south would not budge after one of his officers was killed.

Since the Saigon commanders refused to move, Colonel Vann, the senior American adviser, induced the South Vietnamese command to drop a paratroop battalion, saying it should descend east of the Vietcong to prevent their getting away when night fell. But the airborne battalion landed to the west, leaving a clear avenue of retreat for the Communists. The government was left with sixty-one killed and 100 wounded. The Vietcong vanished in the darkness, leaving only three bodies.

As President Johnson was gearing up to commit American combat troops to Vietnam after he had won the November 1964 presidential election, Americans got other lessons on the kind of war they were getting into. Unfortunately, the U.S. military did not heed them.

At Bienhoa air base, twelve miles north of Saigon, a squadron of American B-57 jet bombers was lined up on the runway. Before dawn on November 1, 1964, a shower of mortar rounds landed on the tarmac, fuel tanks, and buildings, destroying six B-57s, damaging twenty other aircraft, exploding tanks, and killing five Americans and two Vietnamese and wounding a hundred other people. Search parties rushed out but the mortars and the Vietcong had vanished.

On Christmas Eve, 1964, two VC soldiers planted a bomb in the Brinks Hotel, which housed American officers, in central Saigon. In the ensuing explosion, two Americans died and fifty-eight were injured. The event demonstrated that no place in Vietnam was safe, a point reinforced on January 2, 1965, when Vietcong cut to pieces two South Vietnamese ranger companies armed with tanks in an ambush in a rubber plantation about forty miles southeast of Saigon.

On the night of February 6, 1965, a hail of mortar rounds and automatic-weapons fire landed on U.S. special forces and military advisers billets and aircraft at Camp Holloway, three miles from Pleiku in the central highlands. Eight Americans died, a hundred were wounded, and ten U.S. aircraft were destroyed. Again nearly all the Communists escaped, the body of only one being found.

American military commanders wanted to carry out "search-and-destroy" missions from the outset. They maintained the belief, articulated by Lieutenant General Lionel C. McGarr, chief of the U.S. Army's advisory group in Vietnam

1960–62, that the objective was to "find, fix, fight, and finish the enemy."[3]

This was identical to the army's mission in conventional war, and American commanders never overcame the conviction that "finishing" the enemy in battle was their goal. Hence the early emphasis on "body counts," or the numbers of Vietcong (or presumed VC) dead discovered after an engagement—since this was all commanders could point to as positive gains from any firefight. Body counts meant attrition warfare and the army's purpose came to be to force the enemy to quit by wearing him down. But Ho Chi Minh, Giap, and the other Communist leaders were prepared to lose ten soldiers to one American, in the conviction that the American people would not sustain even that ratio of losses indefinitely and would demand withdrawal before the Communists became exhausted. Attrition warfare worked against Americans, not for them.

The search-and-destroy objective of the U.S. Army came into immediate conflict with the army's obligation to defend the many army and air force bases in Vietnam. By the beginning of 1966 about half of American combat forces were protecting base areas and lines of communication. The proportion of static defensive troops never went below 40 percent.[4]

The military also needed large numbers of service troops to deliver the vast amounts of ammunition, fuel, and other supplies it required and to maintain and repair the vast numbers of vehicles, aircraft, and weapons it employed. American forces thus were dispersed over the country at heavily de-

3. Ibid., 57.
4. Kolko, 166.

fended bases. Because of these commitments, Americans and the Saigon army were able to deploy no more actual fighting men than the Vietcong and North Vietnamese, whose total army was only one-fourth as large.[5] So hamstrung, the Americans assumed a largely passive role, unable to project overwhelming force into prolonged active campaigns of their own and forced to respond to the initiatives of the enemy.

The principal purpose of the great array of American equipment was to deliver extremely heavy firepower. But this firepower was largely wasted, due to the fact that the Communists would not wait around to be pounded by American shells and missiles. U.S. forces might "find" Communist units, but they could seldom "fix, fight, and finish" them. As a consequence, the war quickly degenerated into a stalemate.

The lesson this teaches us today is that guerrilla warfare, though it cannot oust a conventional force, can create a military impasse, which ultimately leads to a political settlement. In almost all cases, the settlement is against the country wielding the conventional army. The reason for this is that the guerrillas can continue at a bearable output of treasure and lives, whereas the outside power is forced into high financial expenditures and, over time, cannot justify to its people why it is continuing to incur human losses without resolving the conflict.

The only way to defeat the Communists was by winning "the hearts and minds" of the South Vietnamese people, as a

5. In 1968, when the United States had 543,000 men in Vietnam, only 80,000 were actual combat troops. See Krepinevich, 197; Kolko, 184.

popular slogan went, and thereby causing them to withdraw their support from the Vietcong.

The Saigon government gave lip service to this concept, but refused to provide the people with real improvements, like land reform to reduce high rents for farmland.[6]

The government instituted a "strategic hamlets" program to move peasants into protected villages safe from the VC. But this program crashed on the reef of widespread government perfidy, especially stealing by officials of funds earmarked to build the hamlets and to compensate the peasants for work they did or losses they suffered. It also failed because the peasants were uprooted by force from localities where their forebears had lived for centuries, and they hated the strategic hamlets and abandoned them as quickly as possible.

Winning the hearts and minds of the people became an important goal of the United States. Many critics complained that the Americans should have done more, concentrating most of their resources on turning the people away from the Communists and to the Saigon government. But it is false to think that foreigners can convince the people of another country to adopt policies and beliefs they espouse. Programs must be 99 percent local if they are going to succeed. If people respond, it will be to the arguments of their

6. Ten percent of the people in the South Vietnamese central lowlands and 44 percent in the Mekong delta were landless tenants. In the central lowlands an additional 58 percent rented half or more of the land they farmed, in the Mekong delta, 28 percent. Neither possessed security of tenure. Average rents in the lowlands were 50 percent of the anticipated gross crop, in the delta, 34 percent. The Vietminh worked to reduce landlessness, high rents, high taxes, and indebtedness. They set up local courts that tried to set maximum interest rates and replace the regressive land tax system with a progressive income tax. See Shafer, 264.

own leaders, in their own idiom, and in their own tradition.

This was why winning the hearts and minds of the South Vietnamese was impossible: the country's elites were opposed to reform and blocked it. As an American diplomat, U. Alexis Johnson, wrote in 1962: "The measures we advocate may strike at the very foundations of these aspects of a country's social structure and domestic economy on which rests the basis of the government's control." The aim of South Vietnam's rulers and elites was to preserve their power and privilege, not to improve the lot of the common people.[7]

The memory of what the Chinese, despite their inferior weapons, were able to do in Korea to stop American forces remained vivid to U.S. leaders. When President Johnson decided to send U.S. combat troops into South Vietnam in 1965, he rejected military brass proposals to invade North Vietnam as well because he knew the Chinese would not tolerate American forces on their southern frontier—any more than they would tolerate American forces along the Yalu River in Korea opposite Chinese Manchuria. Thus, Johnson conceded North Vietnam as a sanctuary from invasion (though not from bombing).

At the same time, Johnson refused to permit direct American military intervention in Laos and Cambodia for fear of being labeled by the rest of the world as an aggressor and neocolonialist. Although he and his successor Richard M. Nixon secretly violated this rule (and Nixon invaded Cambodia openly in 1970, as U.S. involvement in Vietnam was winding down), these two states also provided sanctuaries for the Vietnamese Communists.

As a consequence, North Vietnam served as a reliable

7. Ibid., 119–20.

source of war supplies and troop reinforcements to the south, while Laos and Cambodia, through which the Ho Chi Minh Trail ran, served as conduits for supplies and men to be delivered into South Vietnam. Also of great importance: Communist troops at any time could withdraw to safety at bases in the mountains of both countries.

The Communist forces in South Vietnam required only a few tons of supplies a day, since they procured most of their food, clothing, and much of their armament locally. However, the supplies (and the men) that came down the Ho Chi Minh Trail were vital to the success of the Communist military effort. Although American aircraft bombed the trail repeatedly, it was camouflaged so well and repaired so swiftly that they were never able to break it.

Admiral Thomas H. Moorer, chairman of the Joint Chiefs of Staff 1970–74, points out that logistics—or the delivery of food, ammunition, fuel, and other supplies—is the key to victory or defeat in all conflicts.

American air power was able to disrupt the flow of supplies in the Persian Gulf War of 1991, and essentially leave Iraqi armies unable to fight for more than a short time—until stored up supplies ran out. "There was no Ho Chi Minh Trail in Iraq," Admiral Moorer says, "just dusty roads with trucks and other targets in the open and advertising their presence."[8]

This summarizes an essential fact about warfare: where a power can halt an enemy's flow of supplies, it can eliminate the enemy's resistance. Where it cannot, and when the enemy refuses to meet its opponent head-on and can get away at will, the enemy cannot be defeated.

8. Letter to author from Admiral Moorer, January 23, 1994.

TWELVE

Defeating the American Colossus

T HE COMMUNISTS in Vietnam took advantage of the belief of the American military that the best way to win a war is to engage the enemy in violent battles. In such battles, the much more numerous, powerful, and sophisticated U.S. weapons could overwhelm the fewer, less-advanced weapons of the enemy.

The top Red general, Vo Nguyen Giap, baited the American commander, General William C. Westmoreland, with a prize he could not resist: an openly committed North Vietnamese regular army division that intended to fight head-to-head battles with the Americans.[1] Giap deployed these regulars in the heavily forested, sparsely inhabited mountains of central Vietnam near the Cambodian border. And he made threatening gestures that he was going to send the division straight to the sea, and cut South Vietnam in half.

It was the kind of war American generals dreamed about: an enemy who could be found, fixed, fought and finished.

1. Coleman, 51; Moore and Galloway, 49.

The Americans were certain to win such set-piece engagements. General Westmoreland expected to use "search-and-destroy" tactics, exploiting the vastly superior American mobility and firepower to shatter the enemy formations. Thereafter, troops would mop up the remnants. It was a strategy of attrition, to wear down the enemy. Westmoreland believed Hanoi would abandon the war when losses became great.

Thus, after President Johnson committed American combat troops to South Vietnam in the spring of 1965, Westmoreland planned to send forces into the central highlands and block the Communists before they could embark on an offensive. He thereby played into the hands of Hanoi.

Giap and other Communist commanders had no illusions that their regular divisions could stand toe to toe with the American army and slug it out. Their purpose in brandishing their regulars in the central highlands was to entice the Americans. They wanted to hold U.S. troops in this extremely difficult, broken country, so the Vietcong could concentrate on the populated areas and remove them from control of the Saigon government.

Giap believed that despite inevitable losses of manpower in collisions with the Americans, the basic structure of the North Vietnamese army would remain intact, as fresh troops would then replace those lost. In this way, the North Vietnamese army could distract the U.S. Army in inconclusive battles along the frontiers. These would cause a steady drain of casualties and sap U.S. resolve to continue the war.[2]

Westmoreland and other military brass, seeing evidence of North Vietnamese regular forces in the highlands, concluded that the Communists were moving everywhere in

2. Kolko, 179, 183; Krepinevich, 167, 192.

190   *THE FUTURE OF WARFARE*

South Vietnam to the open war phase of their operations, in which conventional formations would challenge the Americans and South Vietnamese directly in head-to-head battles, and attempt to reach a decision in the war.

This was an error in part because it assumed that the move represented an irrevocable strategic change, when in fact the Communists could move back to guerrilla war at any time the costs became too heavy in stand-up battles. It also was an error because Communist military leaders challenged the Americans with their field forces only to pull U.S. troops into the highlands. In the war as a whole, they continued to emphasize small, hit-and-run guerrilla operations. For example, there were thirty-two attacks by Communist battalions (300–600 men) in the second six months of 1964, and only twenty-eight in the first six months of 1965. Battalion attacks represented quite large operations by guerrilla standards, and most such engagements were by smaller units. By 1967, 96 percent were by companies (100–200 men) or smaller detachments.[3]

The Communists thus always maintained the initiative. They could refuse battle or accept it on their own terms, choosing conditions that gave them advantage, adjusting the scope and intensity of the war as they saw fit, and keeping their casualties at a level they could sustain. Consequently, the American strategy of attrition never worked, because the United States could not force the Communists to do battle. A study in 1967, for example, showed that the Communists, not the Americans or South Vietnamese, initiated 88 percent of all engagements.[4]

3. Krepinevich, 161, 192.
4. Ibid., 188.

The American search-and-destroy tactical system also was immensely counterproductive. The basic plan was for U.S. troops to make contact with the enemy, then withdraw, so bombers, attack helicopters, and artillery could blast the enemy. As one American general described the procedure, "You don't fight this fellow rifle to rifle. You locate him and back away. Blow the hell out of him and then police up."[5]

This practice was incredibly expensive and unbelievably destructive, but not usually of Vietcong or North Vietnamese soldiers, who normally were able to get away before the bombs began to land.

American forces exploded nearly 15 million tons of munitions during the Vietnam War, twice the total used by the United States in all of World War II. A policy that encouraged lavish use of explosives also led to indiscriminate use. Often Americans attacked localities without more than a suspicion that the enemy was there. Many thousands of innocent civilians died or were injured. This was especially true because—as Americans became increasingly frustrated with VC elusiveness—any village from which fire came or was suspected might be shattered.

Frustration led to abuses, the most terrible of which was the massacre of up to 400 women, children, and old men in the village of May Lai by a company of the U.S. Americal Division on March 16, 1968.[6] The effect of search-and-destroy was directly contrary to the American intent: shelling and bombing alienated the population and provided the Vietcong with an excellent propaganda issue.[7]

5. Kolko, 179.

6. See Michael Bilton and Kevin Sim, *Four Hours in May Lai* (New York: Viking, 1992).

7. Krepinevich, 81, 198–200.

In the fall of 1965, one North Vietnamese division, along with a Vietcong detachment, fought the U.S. 1st Cavalry Division (Airmobile) in the central highlands west of Pleiku. The strategy and tactics the Communists employed in these engagements constitute a microcosm of the war in Vietnam and dramatize how a weaker power can hold a stronger power at bay and force the war into a standoff.

Nevertheless, General Westmoreland and his operations chief, General William Dupuy, concluded that the 1st Cavalry Division won its engagements because the Communist "body count" was higher than the American toll. This, to them, signified that the attrition strategy was working, when in fact the Communists took losses they could easily sustain, while 1st Cavalry gained little—the Communists forcing the division into a passive role of responding to their initiatives, with one-third of its power devoted to guarding its rear base at An Khe, fifty miles east of Pleiku, "a fort in the middle of Indian Country."[8]

The Communist division, organized as a "field force," was located in and around Chu Pong, a limestone massif full of springs, 2,400 feet above sea level and 1,200 feet above the surrounding rolling plateau. Chu Pong touches the Cambodian border and is about thirty-five miles southwest of Pleiku. The field force was commanded by Brigadier General Chu Hoy Man, and consisted of three North Vietnamese regiments (32d, 33d, and 66th), plus a Vietcong main force battalion (H-15), and attached mortars and antiaircraft (AA) guns—about 10,000 men. Each regiment left North Vietnam with 2,200 soldiers but lost about 20 percent of its strength from the rigors of infiltration. The 32d Regiment

8. Ibid., 169; Coleman, 64; Moore and Galloway, 26.

arrived at Chu Pong in July 1965. The other elements were still walking down the Ho Chi Minh Trail.[9]

General Man opened the campaign to draw in the Americans by sending the 32d Regiment in late July 1965 to surround Duc Co on highway 19, an outpost thirty-three miles west of Pleiku and thirteen miles north of Chu Pong. Duc Co was garrisoned by thirteen American special forces soldiers and about 400 Montagnards, or mercenaries from mountain tribes. The Saigon army sent its Airborne Brigade to Duc Co by helicopter on August 3, but could not advance against well-entrenched Communist soldiers surrounding Duc Co. It and the camp began to run out of supplies, because air drops landed mostly on North Vietnamese-held ground.

General Man's purpose in besieging Duc Co was not to capture it, but to lure a relief column so he could ambush it. On August 9 he succeeded. An armored task force left Pleiku on route 19. The 32d Regiment assaulted the convoy about four miles east of Duc Co, but could not destroy it because the government forces were protected by American-made M-41 tanks (carrying 76mm guns) and M-113 armored personnel carriers (APCs). The task force conducted sweeps around Duc Co, but they were fruitless since General Man had pulled his regiment back to Chu Pong. The Communist attacks had failed, but their boldness had alarmed American and Saigon commanders.

General Man now raised the ante. The 33d Regiment arrived on September 10, 1965, and he ordered a two-regiment movement against another American-Montagnard outpost at Plei Me, twenty-five miles south of Pleiku. It was

9. Details of operations around Pleiku July–November 1965 are drawn from Coleman and Moore and Galloway.

the first time two Communist regiments had been deployed in a single operation in South Vietnam. General Man planned another "lure and ambush" project. The 33d Regiment assaulted Plei Me on the night of October 19, while the 32d Regiment set up a trap on the dirt road connecting Plei Me with route 14 and Pleiku.

The Plei Me attack was extremely violent. Automatic weapons, 82mm mortars, 75mm recoilless rifles and rocket launchers bombarded the compound, destroying several bunkers, while sappers blew a hole in the razor wire outer fence with dynamite. The Communist commander deliberately limited an infantry assault through the opening to a size to make the defenders believe they were about to be overrun but not enough to do so. The assaulting Communist soldiers died in a hail of gunfire.

An American C-123 aircraft dropped flares to permit a flight of U.S. bombers to blast the periphery of the camp with napalm and bombs. But most North Vietnamese soldiers were so close to the wire fence they escaped. At daylight continuous sorties of U.S. bombers began pounding the enemy, causing many casualties, but costing four bombers, an attack helicopter, and seven C-123 supply ships destroyed from ground fire.

Meanwhile the 32d Regiment ambushed the South Vietnamese relief column armed with tanks and APCs on October 23 about eighteen miles south of Pleiku in densely forested terrain. The tanks and APCs beat off the attack, but not before much damage had been done. The ferocity of the 32d Regiment's assaults so stunned the column commander that he refused to move for two days—until 1st Cavalry artillery, dropped by helicopter nearby, delivered shell concentrations just ahead of the column as it crept on to Plei Me.

The North Vietnamese staged one assault against the tanks and APCs at Plei Me, causing many to be killed and wounded, but then began withdrawing back to Chu Pong.

The 1st Cavalry Division's commander, Brigadier General Harry W. O. Kinnard, figured he could catch enemy troops on the move away from Plei Me and the ambush site and General Westmoreland immediately gave his approval to go after them. 1st Cavalry was the only division in the U.S. Army that was fully mobile by helicopters and Kinnard committed his 1st Brigade to the first search-and-destroy mission in which helicopters would be used to lift troops to close with the enemy.

Search-and-destroy was to commence by dispersing helicopters over a wide region to conduct intensive hunts for the North Vietnamese. Some search troops also were to disperse, dropping by UH-1 Huey-D lift helicopters ("slicks") into small open areas (landing zones or LZs) in the forest, then patrolling outward.[10] When soldiers or choppers discovered enemy soldiers, a "rapid-reaction force" at a rear base or LZ was to land on or near them to bring them to battle. The infantry would be supported by machine gun- and rocket-firing helicopter Huey-B gunships ("hogs") and air force bombers. The idea also was to drop 105mm howitzers (range 13,000 meters) into nearby landing zones by medium-lift CH-47 Chinook choppers to provide artillery support.

10. There were numerous small open spaces in the forest, caused by slash-and-burn farming methods of the mountain tribesmen. They would cut trees and other vegetation in a small area, burn it, cultivate crops in the clearing for several years, then allow it to go back to forest, meanwhile cutting another clearing elsewhere.

The North Vietnamese had not expected to be spied on from the air so accurately and the choppers caught many of them in the open. Foliage in many places was light because it was the dry season. 1st Cavalry chopper crews also had developed an extremely effective attack system. When a gunship saw a group of enemy, it "rolled in hot [fast]," firing machine guns on the first run, then pulled up in a steep bank, causing the chopper to skid sideways, presenting one of the two door machine gunners a clear shot before the chopper rolled back on another firing run. Few exposed enemy got away from such an attack.

The first major American success occurred on November 1, when helicopters spotted men by a stream west of Plei Me, and a platoon, dropped into an LZ nearby, walked in and seized a North Vietnamese hospital, killing fifteen and capturing forty-three. A small force from a passing 33d Regiment battalion struck the Americans to cover the battalion's retreat, killing seven and wounding nineteen, then breaking contact and getting away itself.

Over the next several days, 1st Brigade forces fell into several firefights with small detachments of North Vietnamese retreating westward. None was decisive, but all offered lessons about the skill of the enemy in fighting or disengaging when he wanted to. Unfortunately, few Americans were paying attention.

On November 4, for example, the point man of a company on a search mission spotted a flash of khaki uniform by the Tae River, about five miles northeast of the hospital. The point man opened fire with his M-16 automatic rifle—and was riddled by a violent response from numerous positions along the river. The American company assaulted the river line. The North Vietnamese fought hard for a short period, then vanished, revealing why they had engaged the Americans: a North Vietnamese regimental supply dump, stacked with weapons and ammunition. In the brief encounter, the enemy killed four Americans and wounded fifteen. Following their doctrine, the North Vietnamese refused to hold a position, even one as valuable as the arms cache. Their job was to strike as hard as they could, then get away. They knew a determined defense would bring in gunships, fighter-bombers, and artillery—and cause many North Vietnamese casualties.

General Kinnard replaced the 1st Brigade with the 3d Brigade, under Colonel Thomas W. (Tim) Brown. The brigade spent several days searching between Plei Me and the north-south route 14 about twelve miles east, but found no enemy.

Meanwhile, the Vietcong detachment had been moving up on the 3d Brigade headquarters and helicopter laager or forward base at Catecka tea plantation, about eight air miles southwest of Pleiku. On the night of November 12, 1965, it struck, dropping a hundred 60mm and 82mm mortar rounds on Catecka, trying to hit the choppers and the fuel dump. Although the dump remained intact and no chopper was destroyed, nearly all ships were hit, while seven men died, and twenty-three were wounded. Vietcong infantry staged a strong demonstration against the west side of the base perimeter, then faded away in about forty-five minutes, leaving six dead bodies, after gunships silenced the mortars and stopped the ground assault.

The attack demonstrated the vulnerability of American positions to sneak attacks, leading commanders to keep substantial portions of their combat strength guarding their "forts" in "Indian Country."

Colonel Brown, commander of 1st Brigade, realized that the enemy was likely to be in force in the vicinity of the Chu Pong massif. On November 13, he ordered Lieutenant Colonel Harold C. Moore to locate a landing zone near Chu Pong and drop the 450 men of his 1st Battalion, 7th Cavalry, into it and search for enemy troops. To give the battalion artillery support, two batteries (twelve 105mm howitzers) landed at LZ Falcon, about five miles northeast.

Early on November 14, Moore, with his company commanders, reconnoitered the region by helicopter and found an open space, named X-ray, at the foot of Chu Pong and about fourteen miles southwest of Plei Me. X-ray was large enough for ten birds at a time to land. It was oval, about a hundred yards wide, and covered with waist-high yellowed elephant grass. In the center was a small grove of trees and a giant anthill, ten feet high, hard as concrete. To the west was a dry creek bed. Just beyond a ridge sloped up sharply to the crest of Chu Pong.

Brown allocated to Moore sixteen of the brigade's twenty-four helicopters, enough to bring in one company at a time from Plei Me. The choppers dropped the lead company, Captain John D. Herren's Bravo (B), then quickly lifted off to pick up Alpha or A Company under Captain Ramon A. (Tony) Nadal. Moore set up his battalion command post at the giant anthill.

Red General Chu Hoy Man's outposts spotted the American choppers landing right at the North Vietnamese doorstep. Dispersed along the eastern face of Chu Pong was the 33d Regiment, now reduced by losses to a composite battalion, perhaps 500 men. In addition, on Chu Pong were two battalions of the 66th Regiment, plus headquarters, in all about 1,100 men. Man ordered the 33d to attack and by noon it was in position.

Captain Herren led Bravo Company across the dry creek bed and up the finger ridge leading to the top of Chu Pong. Lieutenant Alan E. Devney's 1st Platoon was slightly ahead of Lieutenant Henry T. Herrick's 2d Platoon on the right, and in front of the 3d Platoon, under Lieutenant Dennis J. Deal. Devney's men ran straight into withering small-arms fire of the North Vietnamese assault force, which wounded several men and pinned the platoon down. Herrick's 2d Platoon, hurrying to Devney's assistance, moved too far northward and was isolated.

Meanwhile, the first elements of Captain Robert H. Edwards's Charlie or C Company were landing, as North Vietnamese mortar rounds began feeling out the LZ for American positions. Colonel Moore kept Charlie Company as reserve temporarily and ordered Captain Nadal's Alpha Company to help Herren. Alpha, moving up on Herren's left, came under fierce fire in the dry creek bed from advancing enemy troops. They killed one platoon commander and his sergeant, and though beaten back by Alpha fire, continued flanking the American left.

Artillery and air force spotters in helicopters over X-ray directed fire and air strikes on the lower portions of Chu Pong, then ringed the landing zone with continuous fire and bombings. Enemy gunners on Chu Pong challenged every low pass by American fighter-bombers, hitting an A1E propeller-driven Skyraider, which crashed north of X-ray, the pilot dying. The shelling and bombing appeared to have little effect on the North Vietnamese, who infiltrated the landing zone itself and began lacing it with fire.

The lead elements of Delta or D Company were landing. Two North Vietnamese with AK-47 automatic rifles popped out of the grass and sprayed the chopper carrying the company commander, Captain Louis R. LeFebvre, killing his radio operator. LeFebvre sprinted for the tree line to the north of the LZ, yelling for his men to follow. There he and his troops ran into another storm of fire, which killed another radio operator, and wounded LeFebvre and one of his lieutenants.

When Moore ordered in the last parts of his battalion, enemy fire disabled two helicopters. Wounded piled up at the battalion CP, although several slicks piloted by brave men endured the fire storm and carried out a number of wounded.

Heavy American weapons had beaten back the first thrusts from Chu Pong, but the battalion was being pressed relentlessly by a disciplined, highly motivated enemy who could shoot extremely well. Herrick's cut-off platoon could not move. If a man raised an elbow, a bullet struck. In midafternoon Lieutenant Herrick died, and shortly after, his platoon sergeant. Now eight men were dead and twelve wounded, leaving only seven. Sergeant Clyde E. Savage saved the survivors by calling in artillery concentrations, some landing only twenty-five yards from the tiny perimeter.

Colonel Moore ordered an assault to rescue Herrick's platoon. To prepare the way, forward observers called in an intense artillery barrage. The North Vietnamese, however, had spent the previous hour digging into the ground and most survived the shells. The Americans had gone only fifty yards when they were met by a storm of fire which killed or wounded several. Moore reluctantly ordered his troops to withdraw.

Enemy forces probed the American perimeter repeatedly during the night of November 14, 1965. Making plans for the next day, General Man, the enemy commander, alerted 8th Battalion of the 66th Regiment to be prepared to attack, and directed the H-15 Vietcong battalion, well south of X-ray, to move north and make contact with the Americans.

Colonel Brown, 1st Brigade commander, directed Alpha Company of 2d Battalion, 7th Cavalry, to land at X-ray early on the morning of November 15. His main reinforcement for X-ray, Lieutenant Colonel Robert Tully's 2d Battalion, 5th Cavalry, landed during the night at a clearing, Victor, about two miles southeast of X-ray and was to move overland to the perimeter early in the morning.

Colonel Moore's priority remained to rescue Herrick's isolated platoon, but his forces ran directly into a North Vietnamese company advancing on its hands and knees. The enemy commander had positioned his force so close to the Americans that U.S. artillery and air strikes were not effective.

The North Vietnamese disregarded their losses and kept pressing forward, engaging some Americans in hand-to-hand fighting. About 9 A.M. the fire slackened on the LZ, permitting Alpha 2/7 to land. The North Vietnamese began withdrawing, using snipers tied in trees to cover their retreat. The Americans counted their losses. Charlie Company had suffered most, losing thirty men killed and forty wounded in the three-hour fight. Shortly after noon Tully's battalion (2/5) arrived at the southern edge of X-ray after having received only sporadic resistance. Tully's men moved out to rescue Herrick's platoon. By this time all the enemy except snipers had departed, and the Americans evacuated survivors to the LZ.

The night of November 15 was similar to the night before, with numerous small enemy probes and one company-sized attack that was beaten off. Shortly after dawn, American patrols went out. It was apparent that the overnight attacks had held the Americans in place while the bulk of the enemy had withdrawn out of range of fire. The Americans had lost 70 killed and 121 wounded. They counted 834 enemy dead, and estimated 500 more dead and countless wounded.

On November 17, U.S. forces abandoned the LZ. The same day, however, 8th Battalion of the 66th North Vietnamese Regiment ambushed most of 2d Battalion of the 7th Cavalry while the Americans were marching overland to LZ Albany, on the Drang River about four miles north of X-ray. The ambush came near to being a massacre, the Americans losing 151 killed, 121 wounded, and four missing, although the North Vietnamese lost about 400 killed before they withdrew.

Since most American strikes were by helicopter, not on the ground, U.S. forces seldom got themselves in positions where they were exposed so flagrantly to ambush as at Albany. Consequently commanders saw Albany as an aberration and not as a pattern for the war as a whole.

The last engagement around the Chu Pong massif occurred at 5 P.M. on November 18, when the H-15 Vietcong battalion struck an LZ three miles northeast of X-ray, Columbus, and continued the attack until about midnight. The enemy disabled two choppers and killed three Americans and wounded thirteen, but could do little more against U.S. artillery fire and air strikes.

On November 19 choppers pulled Americans out of both LZ Albany and LZ Columbus. The campaign was over.

The Americans listed about 1,300 enemy dead, as opposed to 224 American dead. Perhaps the Americans were overzealous in their count of the enemy, perhaps not. But it made little difference. To General Westmoreland and other top leaders, the results of X-ray particularly seemed to prove that the Americans could win a war of attrition rapidly. After all, enemy losses at X-ray seemed to be at least ten times the American losses. Yet ominous lessons taught at X-ray were not learned.

The first lesson was that U.S. forces had responded only to enemy action. They had initiated no more than the strike at X-ray itself. Everything else had been reaction to North Vietnamese moves. The second was that the enemy troops had disengaged precisely when and how they wanted, holding the Americans in place until they got away. This demonstrated that, despite immensely superior American firepower, the Reds could determine how long they wanted to remain in contact and how many casualties they were willing to accept.

The Americans taught the North Vietnamese the third lesson: that U.S. military power indeed was frightful and they could not endure it indefinitely. The Communists learned to avoid this firepower. They soon reverted to their tried-and-true strategy of guerrilla or semiguerrilla strikes by small forces.

They challenged the Americans directly in occasional local fights, but embarked on an open campaign against Americans only once more, the Tet offensive, beginning on January 31, 1968, when nearly 70,000 Communist soldiers surged into more than a hundred South Vietnamese cities, including Saigon.

A remarkable, and seldom noted, aspect about the Tet offensive was that South Vietnamese troops, the Vietcong, carried the main burden. North Vietnamese regulars created diversions to continue the primary Communist strategy of drawing American combat forces away from the populated regions into remote areas where their power would be wasted. This was highly successful and symbolized by the siege of Khe Sanh, a base in the mountains near Laos and the demilitarized zone along the 17th parallel.

There were 6,000 American and South Vietnamese troops at Khe Sanh when the siege commenced on January 21, 1968, ten days before Tet. They faced two North Vietnamese divisions, about 20,000 men. Westmoreland sent more troops and at the height of the siege 50,000 Americans were tied down at Khe Sanh, making things easier for the VC attacking in the south. The siege ended in March 1968, not broken by the United States, but by the North Vietnamese, its diversionary purpose fulfilled.[11]

Though Tet failed, it demonstrated that the Communists had not been defeated, and brought on final American disillusionment with the war—as well as the recognition by President Johnson that his hopes for victory were unfounded. This led to his consequent refusal to stand for reelection.

But long before, at X-ray, in the first major clash between Americans and North Vietnamese, U.S. commanders had been shown the limits of American military power. The Communists absorbed their losses and went on, undeterred. The American people paid little attention to the number of enemy killed and wounded. But the losses sustained by U.S. forces at and around X-ray made a profound impact. As the enemy could not be induced to give up and continued to kill and maim U.S. troops, the American people at length refused to support the war.

11. Young, 216–7, 221.

THIRTEEN

Winning or Avoiding Future Wars

F OR TWO GENERATIONS the United States was the free world's watchdog, alertly patrolling the periphery of the Iron and Bamboo Curtains, barking loudly at every doubtful noise or movement, and attacking fiercely everywhere it thought it saw danger.

The Cold War had a marvelous simplicity about it. The Soviet Union or China managed everything on one side of the fence; the United States more or less managed everything on the other side. Whatever the actual attitude of other Western powers, they mostly lined up behind the United States, or kept their views to themselves so as to maintain a solid front against the Eastern bloc. The Communist satellites in Europe likewise fell in line behind the Kremlin, willingly or unwillingly, although Red China and the Soviet Union were able to keep up their pretense of unity only from 1949 to about 1960.

The major East-West bones of contention were in the Third World, and even there the two sides were able to come to a rough understanding or agree to disagree without coming to direct blows. The constant fear of nuclear holocaust had a capacity for concentrating the attention of leaders everywhere. This led them to quash the ambitions of potential troublemakers who might set East and West on an unstoppable course toward disaster.

Today the bipolar world is gone. Disputes suppressed for decades by both sides in order to present a united front now rage uncontrolled. With the planet no longer cleanly divided into "us" and "them," leaders are distracted by a thousand conflicting claims and ambitions. We inhabit a much more disorderly world. Disputes within and between nations are frequently violent, divisive, and dangerous.

No existing international institution can take the place of East-West tension to resolve or to paper over these disputes. The North Atlantic Treaty Organization has too many cooks in its kitchen and too many doubts about its new role as an alliance without an enemy. It demonstrated in the war in Bosnia that it is unprepared to take on the job of international peacemaker. Many people want to foist the task on the United Nations. The UN has an important role, especially as a peacekeeper once two opposing sides have come to a ceasefire. But the UN reflects the babble of disparate voices and views that cause internal and international conflicts in the first place. The alliances and antagonisms, loyalties and prejudices of its members leave it scarcely capable of being the objective arbiter the world needs.

Other people want the United States to expand its watchdog job to include the whole world. Not only would it be an intolerable burden on the United States to take responsibility for everything, everywhere, but other nations will not accept the United States in that role.

Yet there is a vital task for the United States, a responsibility no other nation can assume. The United States occupies a special place because it possesses the world's greatest military and economic strength and, as we saw in chapter 1, its strategic imperatives force it to oppose the rise of another hegemonic world power, and to keep vital commodities from being cornered by a single nation or alliance. The United States has few special biases. Its principal one is to prevent any threat in the Western Hemisphere. As a consequence, the United States can become the "honest broker" in international disputes.

The German "iron chancellor," Otto von Bismarck, coined the phrase "honest broker" in 1878 at the Congress of Berlin, which he guided and which resolved an earlier Balkan crisis. Germany, only recently united and exulting in its status as a great power, had no overriding interests in the Balkans. Being therefore neutral, Bismarck was able to arbitrate the intense competitive interests of Russia, Austria-Hungary, Britain, and Turkey, not to speak of the violent conflicts between the Balkan nations and peoples.

Today the world desperately needs an honest broker. Countries everywhere will resist being ordered around, but they want arbitration by a neutral party who has few axes to grind. The United States can be that arbiter.

A role as honest broker is something new for the United States. Its leaders were thrust into the nonnegotiating rigidity of the Cold War on the heels of World War II, learning little about compromise, or why long-standing economic or social inequities were often more important than ideology in generating conflicts. Before World War II, the United States was constrained in international negotiations because of the fierce isolationist reaction of the American people to the results of World War I. The Depression of the 1930s intensified this isolationism, leading to a high tariff wall that limited trade with other countries and turned the people inward economically and psychologically. Until World War I, American reluctance to venture far beyond the Western Hemisphere led the United States to play only a moderate role on the world stage.[1]

Today the world needs the United States to take the lead in bringing together other responsible powers to resolve issues that the parties involved are unable to settle. With NATO and the United Nations ill-suited to examine international conflicts dispassionately, the time has come for the United States to lead other major powers to take on the task.

Most countries that would resist American pressure will respond willingly to American leadership. If the United States had called another "Congress of Berlin" when Yugoslavia disintegrated, and had brought in Russia, Germany, France, Britain and the powers in the region, a consensus for a settlement could have been reached. If the Serbians then had insisted on embarking on a campaign of "ethnic cleansing" to drive the Moslems of Bosnia out of their lands, the world—and most especially their traditional friends, the Russians—would have turned on them. In that circumstance, massacres of innocent people probably would not have occurred, or they could have been stopped sooner.

World leadership has devolved in a peculiar fashion on

1. Many Americans were unwilling to take on the role of an imperial power after the United States seized the Philippine islands in the Spanish-American War of 1898. This led to promises to grant the Philippines ultimate independence. The United States annexed Guam as a way station to the Philippines. Its annexation of Hawaii served to shield the Western Hemisphere from attack across the Pacific, while its takeover of Puerto Rico was to protect the proposed Panama Canal. Annexation of eastern Samoa made less strategic sense, but it served as a coaling station or base in the south Pacific.

the United States. The principal reason is that much of the planet has embraced the ideals of personal freedom, democracy, market economy, and liberal world trade that the United States espouses. This makes an American role as honest broker more acceptable and more believable. Also, since the United States is the last economic and military superpower, every state that might want to balk knows that our velvet glove of persuasion could conceal an iron fist of force.

This does not mean that the United States must go to war every time it fails to resolve a dispute by negotiation. Most conflicts, even wars, that countries are going to get into will not threaten principal American strategic interests. We would like to stop them because of the human tragedy they cause. But when disputes do not endanger our interests and do not destabilize larger regions, we should not intervene with our troops, whether or not violence occurs. We finally came to this conclusion in Somalia. The Rwandan massacres in April–May 1994 illustrate how complex internal conflicts can erupt before outsiders have any chance of influencing them. In the space of weeks, perhaps 200,000 people had been killed in Rwanda, mainly minority Tutsis by the majority Hutus. In such situations, negotiations may bring about a cease-fire, but not prevent disaster.

The United States can be the world's honest broker, but it cannot be the world's protector. As the syndicated newspaper columnist Stephen Chapman wrote on April 23, 1994, most people who urge American intervention in trouble spots are driven by mere sentiment. "But sentiment," he insisted, "is no basis for establishing policies on when, where, or how to risk American lives and resources."

We cannot intervene everywhere. We should intervene only to protect the nation's strategic imperatives. In most cases, the United States can attain its goals by negotiation and diplomacy. But in some cases it must use force to prevent another power from achieving an advantage—as it prevented Iraq from acquiring control of Persian Gulf oil.

Applying the test of whether an issue affects American strategic imperatives will add great clarity to the force projections and conflict scenarios the U.S. military must train for and be prepared to execute. It also will discourage urges of political leaders—brought on both by sentiment and by ambition—to rush into military adventures that have no connection with protecting the security of the United States.[2]

The United States could reduce much barbarism in the world by becoming an honest broker. The congresses the United States calls or the pressures it exerts with other world powers will not always bring peaceful solutions, but they will

2. This urge can be seen most cogently when President Clinton renewed the most-favored nation (MFN) status of China in May 1994, a decision that preserved the immense and growing trade relationship between the United States and China. Some members of Congress and many groups seeking greater civil rights for Chinese nationals opposed MFN, although ending MFN would not have improved the treatment of Chinese dissidents, while it would have brought fierce Chinese economic retaliation. The United States must distinguish between its strategic imperatives and its aspirations for other countries to adopt human-rights and other policies it follows. Threats to American strategic imperatives may require projections of military force. Threats to the civil rights of another country's people should be dealt with by persuasion and example, not force. Why should repression of dissidents in China be singled out for U.S. action? Many other governments also repress their people. Indeed, American business people working in China made the strongest argument for MFN: that more trade with China will lead to better economic conditions for the Chinese, encouragement of a market economy, and quicker elimination of a command economy directed from the Communist leadership in Beijing. Rigid governmental control is the driving force for repression of citizens. A liberal market economy is the most likely means of bringing forth more freedom for the people.

in more cases than not. Even when they do not, they will isolate the guilty party and make it easier to limit his aggressions. Congresses and united action by responsible powers remain the best devices we possess to resolve disputes short of war.[3]

Countries occasionally throw up leaders like Adolf Hitler in Germany, Benito Mussolini in Italy, Saddam Hussein in Iraq, or Slobodan Milosevic in Serbia who are unreasonable, aggressive, or greedy, or who represent the deep-seated prejudices or aspirations of their peoples. Such leaders drive their countries to war. But they can usually be thwarted if they are challenged when they first act aggressively.

We see Saddam Hussein as a failed aggressor because we stopped him at the start of his expansion. We see Hitler as a monster because we did not. Hitler might never have brought the world to chaos if the United States had joined with Britain and France and threatened war when Germany's army was still feeble and Hitler undertook his first aggressive move, the reoccupation of the demilitarized Rhineland in 1936. But then the United States was weak militarily and

3. Colonel George T. Raach, formerly on the faculty of the National War College, Washington, and since 1994 an associate professor at the Army War College, Carlisle, Pennsylvania, writes: "The position of the U.S. in the eyes of most of the world is a position of leadership. We've had this position since World War II, and it is not based entirely on our military prowess. . . . Our leadership comes as much from moral rectitude and economic prosperity as from military might. We have an aura that is hard to describe but is nevertheless there—at least in the eyes of many beholders. They understand that we won't take on every crisis. They also expect us to step in when really important issues are at stake. . . . If we failed to meet their expectations, our ability to influence subsequent events (and perhaps to prevent the creation of anti-U.S. cartels) would be substantially diminished. . . . We must own up to the fact that we must, on occasion, lead." From letter to author from Colonel Raach, May 17, 1994.

could not project its power into Eurasia. Today the United States is strong, can project its power, and is far less inhibited to take such definitive action than it was then.

Negotiating is all the more important because wars are becoming less useful for forcing peoples to buckle under to outsiders' demands. As we have seen in previous chapters, the history of the last half of this century demonstrates that peoples have taken to heart the teachings of Mao Zedong and are determined to resist foreign powers, even when these powers possess much superior armament. They have showed that there are other ways of winning than by sheer force. Aggressors have had an extremely difficult time winning wars since World War II. This casts great doubt on whether nations should invade other countries except in the most desperate situations.

Internal resistance, primarily by guerrilla warfare, forced France to withdraw from Indochina in 1954 and Algeria in 1962. Similar resistance forced the Soviet Union to get out of Afghanistan in the late 1980s. In both the Korean and Vietnam Wars, the United States, despite unapproachable military power, could not gain victory. The incursion into Somalia in 1992–94 demonstrated both how easy it is for the United States to stumble into conflicts, despite its best intentions, and how the United States cannot win such conflicts, despite its power.

This pattern will probably recur in the future. Determined nations—facing invaders with much-superior forces—will see what Lawrence of Arabia saw in 1916: an army that derives its strength from "an idea" and that moves like a vapor presents little the enemy can hit. This army remains "a thing intangible, invulnerable." We saw in Vietnam how "an idea" played out: the Communists exploited the people's desires for independence, eviction of imperialists, and land reform. Thereby gaining the people's loyalty, they struck blows where they could, withdrew when they had to, and per-servered, until first France, and then the United States, grew weary and withdrew.

The lesson is clear. As opposed to how it acted in Viet-nam, the United States should appraise its enemies and its national interests carefully and objectively. It should try to negotiate peaceful solutions. In many cases the United States will not have to destroy an enemy army or occupy the en-emy's territory in order to achieve negative goals. In other words, leaders should strive for deterrence, not unarguable military victory.

For example, we may use our naval power to restrict the trade of an obstreperous regime, such as we did against the military rulers of Haiti in 1993–94 and against Iraq after the Gulf War. If this is insufficient or if a country has invaded another country where vital U.S. interests are at stake, we may eliminate the military threat by a quick victory, such as Douglas MacArthur achieved against the North Koreans after landing at Inchon in September 1950. Hopefully we will stop there, instead of attempting then to annihilate the enemy. This is how the United States got involved in a war with China—by deciding to go beyond its decisive victory at Inchon and destroy North Korea root and branch, thereby threatening China directly.

But when we face an enemy who refuses to meet Ameri-can power head-on, who draws U.S. forces into his country and embarks on a long war of stalemate or attrition, the United States should remember its wars against the Chinese and the Vietnam Communists and attempt any acceptable solution short of war, choosing invasion as the last resort.

And when we do invade, we should bear in mind that our primary aim is to force the enemy to end his objectionable actions.

The United States may attempt to accomplish this objective by using the following two-stage strategy, a strategy that should apply, in general, to powerful countries invading weaker ones. In the first stage, we would overwhelm the enemy defenses and quickly eliminate organized resistance by regular enemy forces, topple the government (as in Panama in 1989), or disrupt the existing power balance (as in Somalia in 1993). We would immediately bring about the cessation of the country's obnoxious international (not necessarily internal) behavior, and we would seize the principal enemy leaders or drive them under cover. This would be an extremely traumatic and costly experience to the people of the invaded country—one they would not want repeated. At this stage, there would be no organized opposition because the nation's leadership system would have been temporarily paralyzed.

If at this point we were to withdraw our forces, the leaders who would emerge or reemerge would cease international confrontations if only to avoid another invasion. They would be unlikely to improve poor internal conditions, but these conditions would not affect other countries.

If we were to remain as an occupying power, however, the country's leaders would be able to exploit the inherent antagonism of the people to an invader and organize a guerrilla war. If this war had the support of the people as a whole (or even a significant percentage) we might be able to keep our forces in the country, but we would not win and would suffer steady losses. Examples of such a situation may be seen in Northern Ireland and the West Bank of Palestine.

An invasion that ends in early withdrawal rather than occupation may not provide the total victory that some Americans long for in political and military matters. These individuals seek a stark "High Noon" resolution of conflict that may leave bodies spread about the landscape but settles the issue indisputably.

However, when one state seeks to prevent another from following a particular course of action, an attempt at total military defeat may be the wrong tack. International pressure should be the first option. If diplomacy fails, a naval blockade, escalating later, if necessary, to selective air strikes and perhaps limited military action may be more effective than an attempted war of annihilation. Most leaders, when they find their plans are going to be extremely painful and costly to carry out, will abandon them, if only because their people are likely to lose faith in the leaders and their promises.

The likelihood that we will encounter determined opponents who insist on following their goals instead of ours forces us to consider what our national interests are before committing our forces to war. Both of the substantial wars the United States has fought since World War II—in Korea and in Vietnam—could have been limited in one case and avoided in the other if U.S. leaders had examined the facts instead of succumbing to their ambitions or reacting to their fears.

If American leaders had overcome their desire to conquer North Korea, they could have ended the Korean War in October 1950, after the United States had successfully stopped North Korean aggression. What is less well known is that they also could have concluded an armistice with China in July 1951, if they had restrained their anger at China for stopping the American effort to conquer North Korea.

Americans fought on for two years and achieved nothing. What is strangest of all, U.S. leaders doggedly pursued this war despite the fact that they had no plans whatsoever to invade North Korea again and had no strategic goal greater than the Chinese had offered them in July 1951. The Korean War is a large lesson written in our history books for us to be certain of what we want before we fight.

We could have been spared the Vietnam War entirely if American leaders had recognized that intervention, under the conditions of a North Vietnamese sanctuary, made a war impossible to win. In addition, the "falling-domino theory" was utterly wrong and was easily disprovable before we intervened. The Chinese and the Soviets had made it plain at the 1954 Geneva conference that they were perfectly willing to betray their supposed allies, the Vietminh, and they demonstrated that they possessed no vision for expanding into Indochina. If U.S. leaders had studied the situation dispassionately, they would have realized that the conflict in Vietnam was a civil war and represented little international danger.

To make such judgments in the heat of passion and confrontation requires clear vision and a high level of statesmanship. Our elected officials are not likely to have this vision or to manifest such leadership every time. Consequently, we must recognize that we may fall into traps like Vietnam in the future. Hopefully, we will learn from our mistakes and, when we realize anew that we can't conquer people who don't wish to be ruled by us, we will get out quickly. We did this in 1994 in Somalia. If this lesson and the more painful lessons of Korea and Vietnam remain bright in our memories, we may avoid terrible mistakes in the future. If they do not, we will not.

The United States today has three specific military challenges. The first is that it must continue to perfect and build sophisticated weapons for fear other countries will do likewise. The second is that the army must restore movement to the battlefield because modern weapons are so accurate and deadly they threaten to immobilize present heavy forces (see chapter 4). The third is that the United States must reckon with the likelihood that most enemies will avoid its weapons and seek indirect ways, like ambushes or sneak attacks, to strike at its forces.

The United States cannot assume that potential enemies will renounce the most modern weapons because American arms are so greatly superior. The prospects are quite the contrary. In Vietnam the Communists made no attempt to match heavy American weapons like fighter-bombers, helicopters, tanks, and field artillery. But they employed the very best weapons for the close-in kind of combat they pursued, equipping their men with Kalashnikov AK-47 automatic rifles, plus modern machine guns, rocket launchers, mortars, and grenades. In their air war in North Vietnam against American bombers, they deployed sophisticated radar warning systems, Soviet ground-to-air missiles, defensive jet aircraft, and modern antiaircraft guns. Our future enemies will use the most advanced weapons they can build or secure even when they do not try to challenge our weapons superiority as a whole. Their aim will still be to avoid our power and hit us where we are most vulnerable.

Developing a method to restore movement to the battlefield will likely involve greater use of helicopters to deliver light forces at critical enemy points—to destroy enemy artillery and missile emplacements or airfields, for example, thereby preventing these weapons from striking our ground-based tanks, armored personnel carriers and artillery, and permitting these heavy weapons to close with the enemy along with helicopter-borne forces and defeat him.

Enemy forces may employ the same tactics. But we also must be prepared to fight an enemy who strikes, guerrilla-fashion, only at our weaknesses—such as our supply lines, airports, convoys, rear bases, isolated detachments, and cities. Advances in stealth technology that make it more difficult to detect enemy personnel and weapons may make such sneak attacks easier and more deadly. We also may encounter an enemy who combines highly mobile helicopter-borne maneuver forces with traditional guerrilla sneak attacks.

One important point we should remember: there are only two types of war we cannot win. The first is an immobile, defensive struggle such as the one that the Chinese waged against us in the last two years of the Korean War (see chapter 9). Such a war is unlikely to recur because the perpetrator must deploy immense numbers of troops and will suffer enormous losses from American firepower. The second is a guerrilla war in a country we have invaded where the people are hostile. Such a war is much more likely.

As mentioned in chapter 2, Mao Zedong's principles of guerrilla war are valid when applied to a defensive war to deter invasion. We can inflict great damage when we invade another country, but we cannot win a decisive victory if its people are hostile and begin a guerrilla war. In some cases invasion may be justified to stop behavior we oppose. But Mao's principles show that we run great risks of becoming enmeshed in a protracted war if try to achieve a decisive victory. We saw in Vietnam that we cannot.

Though they pose no strategic danger, there will always be pressure from elements within the United States to intervene in countries like Panama or Haiti, where autocracies, oligarchies, or military dictatorships prevent democracy and exploit the people, or in places like Somalia or Rwanda where internal disputes lead to starvation or massacre.

Even if the United States occupies a country whose leaders offend American leaders and forces a new government, it cannot guarantee transformation of that country into a liberal democracy. The conditions that brought on undemocratic conditions in the first place will recur, unless American forces remain as an army of occupation.[4] In that case, they run the risk of generating another Vietnam-type war to oust the foreign invader. American intervention to force other people to be more like ourselves may bring temporary relief but no fundamental change.

If we intervene in response to a vociferous lobby inside the United States, American forces will be diverted from their real strategic imperatives and will suffer losses that can cause grave domestic discord. The body of the American soldier who was dragged by ropes through the streets of Mogadishu, Somalia, in October 1993, should offer a vivid reminder that American leaders cannot force another country to transform itself into an image of the United States.

Although Mao's principles thus have a sobering deterrent effect on American intervention in other countries, they have a positive side as well. For no other country can carry on an aggressive war by using guerrilla tactics. A war without front lines requires the active participation of a friendly pop-

4. U.S. Marines occupied Haiti from 1915 to 1934, during which time the United States imposed a protectorate on the country. The U.S. Navy governed the Dominican Republic from 1916 to 1924. In neither country was the United States able to bring about a democratic government. See Julius W. Pratt, *A History of United States Foreign Policy* (New York: Prentice-Hall, 1955), 422–26, 606, 612.

ulation, and this can be assured only in one's own country, and not in a land that is invaded. Therefore, aggression must be conducted by means of conventional war. Because the United States possesses by far the strongest conventional force on earth, it can defeat any aggressor who invades a friendly country—if it so chooses.

If our politicians assess challenges in light of the limits on American power, they will not impose impossible tasks on our military forces as they did in Vietnam and in Korea. If they look at our possibilities realistically, they will approach disputes less belligerently and more objectively.

Such procedures will require our politicians to concentrate less on pacifying special interests at home and more on rising above their desire for immediate results, favorable headlines, and assuring votes for reelection. They will obligate politicians to analyze the real challenges our country faces.

It's a big order. But it can be done. We need to remember the advice of Theodore Roosevelt, who was president from 1901 to 1909: "Speak softly and carry a big stick." Such a policy will compel us to accept the fact that the United States cannot solve all the world's problems. But it will safeguard our future by preventing us from dissipating our strength in conflicts that arouse our sentiment but do not affect our strategic imperatives. We should reserve our big stick for issues that endanger our national security.

Selected Bibliography

Alexander, Bevin. *Korea: The First War We Lost*. New York: Hippocrene, 1986, 1993.

Alexander, Don W. *Rod of Iron: French Counterinsurgency Policy in Aragon during the Peninsular War*. Wilmington, Dela.: Scholarly Resources, 1985.

Department of the U.S. Army, Headquarters. *Field Manual 100-5 Operations*. Washington, D.C., June 14, 1993.

Asprey, Robert B. *War in the Shadows: The Guerrilla in History*. 2 vols. New York: Doubleday, 1975.

Belfield, Eversley. *The Boer War*. London: Leo Cooper, 1975.

Bergerud, Eric M. *Red Thunder, Tropic Lightning: The World of a Combat Division in Vietnam*. Boulder, Colo.: Westview Press, 1993.

Bilton, Michael, and Kevin Sim. *Four Hours in May Lai*. New York: Viking, 1992.

Bjelajac, S. N. "Guerrilla Operations in Conjunction with Conventional Forces." Department of the Army, deputy chief of staff for military operations, Washington: 1955.

Blank, Stephen. "Afghanistan and Beyond: Reflections on the Future of Warfare." *Small Wars and Insurgencies* 3 (Winter 1992): 217–240.

———. *Afghanistan and Beyond: Reflections on the Future of Warfare*. Strategic Studies Institute, Army War College, 1993.

Buchanan, William J., Lt. Col., and Lt. Col. Robert A. Hyatt. "Guerrilla Vulnerabilities." *Military Review*, Professional Journal of the U.S. Army, 48 (August 1968): 3–40.

Chaliand, Gérard. *Report from Afghanistan*. New York: Viking, 1981.

———, ed. *Guerrilla Strategies*. Berkeley: University of California Press, 1982.

Chinnery, Philip D. *Life on the Line: Stories of Vietnam Air Combat.* New York: St. Martin's Press, 1988.

Clutterbuck, Richard L., Col. "Communist Defeat in Malaya." *Military Review,* 43 (September 1963): 63–78.

Coleman, J. D. *Pleiku.* New York: St. Martin's, 1988.

Coroalles, Anthony M., Maj. "The Master Weapon: The Tactical Thought of J. F. C. Fuller Applied to Future War." *Military Review* 71 (January 1991): 62–72.

Dubik, James M., Lt. Col. "Military Force: Preparing for the Future." *Military Review* 72 (March 1992): 77–83.

Dunnigan, James F., and Raymond M. Macedonia. *Getting It Right: American Military Reforms after Vietnam to the Gulf War and Beyond,* New York: William Morrow, 1993.

Earle, Edward Mead, ed. *Makers of Modern Strategy.* Princeton, N.J.: Princeton University Press, 1943.

Ewald, Johann. *Treatise on Partisan Warfare.* Translated and edited by Robert A. Selig and David C. Skaggs. New York: Greenwood, 1991.

Farwell, Byron. *The Great Anglo-Boer War.* New York: Harper & Row, 1976.

Fields, Rick. *The Code of the Warrior.* New York: HarperCollins, 1991.

Foley, Thomas C., Maj. Gen. "An Armored Force for the Future 2000 and Beyond—Technology." *Armor* 100 (September–October 1991): 3–6; 100 (November–December 1991): 4–6.

Friedman, George, and Meredith Lebard. *The Coming War with Japan.* New York: St. Martin's, 1991.

Fuller, J. F. C. *The Conduct of War, 1789–1961.* New Brunswick, N.J.: Rutgers University Press, 1961.

Garcia, Rudolph N., Capt. "Lettow-Vorbeck, Conventional Army, Guerrilla Army." *Military Intelligence,* U.S. Army Intelligence Center and School, Ft. Huachuca, Ariz., 11 (January–March 1985): 28–33.

Giap, Vo Nguyen. *The Military Art of People's War.* Edited and introduction by Russell Stetler. New York: Monthly Review Press, 1970.

Griffith, James B., Capt. "Guerrilla Warfare in China." *The Cavalry Journal* 50 (September–October 1941): 11–21.

Guerrilla Strategies: An Historical Anthology from the Long March to Afghanistan. Berkeley, Calif.: University Press of California, 1982.

Hasenauer, Heike. "Glimpsing the Future Soldier." *Soldiers* 47 (November 1992): 49–50.

Heymann, Frederick. *John Zizka and the Hussite Revolution*. New York: Russell & Russell, 1955.

Ian, F. W. Beckett, ed. *The Roots of Counter-Insurgency: Armies and Guerrilla Warfare, 1900–1945*. New York: Blandford, 1988.

Isby, David C. *War in a Distant Country, Afghanistan: Invasion and Resistance*. London: Arms and Armour Press, 1989.

Karnow, Stanley. *Vietnam, A History*. New York: Viking, 1983.

Klonis, N. I. *Guerrilla Warfare: Analysis and Projections*. New York: Robert Speller & Sons, 1972.

Kolko, Gabriel. *Anatomy of a War: Vietnam, the United States, and the Modern Historical Experience*. New York: Pantheon, 1985.

Krepinevich, Andrew F., Jr. *The Army and Vietnam*. Baltimore: Johns Hopkins University Press, 1986.

Lawrence, T. E. *The Seven Pillars of Wisdom*. London: Jonathan Cape, 1927; New York: Doubleday, 1935; New York: Anchor Books, 1991. (First published privately 1926.)

Leonard, Robert R. *The Art of Maneuver: Maneuver-Warfare Theory and AirLand Battle*. Novato, Calif.: Presidio, 1991.

Libbey, Miles A., III, and Maj. Patrick A. Putignano. "See Deep, Shoot Deep, UAVs on the Future Battlefield." *Military Review* 71 (February 1991): 38–47.

Lind, William S. *Maneuver Warfare Handbook*. Boulder, Colo.: Westview, 1985.

Macgregor, Douglas A. "Future Battle: The Merging Levels of War." *Parameters,* U.S. Army War College Quarterly, 22 (Winter 1992–93): 33–47.

Mahnken, Thomas G. "Planning U.S. Forces for the Twenty-first Century." *Strategic Review* 20 (Fall 1992): 9–17.

Malkin, Lawrence. "The First Spanish Civil War," *Military History Quarterly,* Winter 1989, 19–29.

von Manstein, Erich. *Lost Victories*. Chicago: Regnery, 1958.

Mao Zedong. *Mao Tse-tung on Guerrilla Warfare*. Translated and introduction by Brig. Gen. Samuel B. Griffith. New York: Praeger, 1961.

McMichael, Scott R. *Stumbling Bear: Soviet Military Performance in Afghanistan*. New York: Brassey's, 1991.

Moore, Harold G., Lt. Gen., and Joseph L. Galloway. *We Were Soldiers Once . . . And Young, Ia Drang—the Battle that Changed the War in Vietnam*. New York: Random House, 1992.

O'Connell, Robert L. *Of Arms and Men: A History of War, Weapons, and Aggression*. New York: Oxford, 1989.

Pakenham, Thomas. *The Boer War*. New York: Random House, 1979.

Paret, Peter, ed. *Makers of Modern Strategy*. Princeton, N.J.: Princeton University Press, 1986.

Persian Gulf War, Conduct of the. Washington, D.C.: Department of Defense, April 1992. Final report to Congress.

Peters, Ralph, Maj.. "The Movable Fortress: Warfare in the 21st Century." *Military Review* 73 (June 1993): 62–72.

Petersen, John L. "Plan for the 21st Century Now." *Proceedings*, U.S. Naval Institute, 117 (August 1991): 49–54.

Pimlott, John, ed. *Guerrilla Warfare*. New York: The Military Press, 1985.

Rommel, Erwin. *The Rommel Papers*. New York: Harcourt, Brace, 1953.

Rothmann, Harry E., Colonel. "The U.S. Army, Strategic Formulation, and Force Planning: Past, Present, Future." Study, Naval War College, Newport, Rhode Island, 1990.

Sarkesian, Sam C. *The New Battlefield: The United States and Unconventional Conflicts*. New York: Greenwood, 1986.

Shafer, D. Michael. *Deadly Paradigms: The Failure of U.S. Counterinsurgency Policy*. Princeton, N.J.: Princeton University Press, 1988.

Shannon, John W., acting secretary of the army, and General Gordon R. Sullivan. *U.S. Army Posture Statement FY94*. Washington, D.C.: Department of the Army, 1993.

"Satellites Manage Future Battlefields," *Signal* 47 (January 1993), Armed Forces Communications and Electronics Association, Fairfax, Va: 58–60.

Simpkin, Richard E. *Race to the Swift: Thoughts on Twenty-first Century Warfare*. Oxford, London: Brassey's Defence Publishers, 1987.

———. *Deep Battle: The Brainchild of Marshal Tuckhachevskii*. Oxford, London: Brassey's Defence Publishers, 1987.

Sullivan, Gordon R., and James M. Dubik. *Land Warfare in the 21st Century*. Carlisle, Pa.: Strategic Studies Institute, Army War College, 1993.

Sun Tzu. *The Art of War*. Edited and foreword by James Clavell. New York: Delacorte Press, 1983.

Swinburn, Sir Richard, Lt. Gen. "Future Armoured Warfare: The Case for the Tank." *RUSI Journal* 137 (June 1992), Royal United Services Institute for Defence Studies, London: 35–37.

Tanham, George K. *Communist Revolutionary Warfare: From the Vietminh to the Viet Cong*, New York: Frederick A. Praeger, 1961.

Taylor, Charles W. *A Concept for a Future Force*. Carlisle, Pa.: Strategic
     Studies Institute, Army War College, 1990.
———. *A World 2010: A New Order of Nations*. Carlisle, Pa.: Strategic
     Studies Institute, Army War College, 1992.
Thies, Wallace J. "A Twenty-first Century Army." *Parameters,* U.S. Army
     War College Quarterly, 21 (Spring 1991): 62–76.
Thompson, Sir Robert, ed. *War in Peace, Conventional and Guerrilla War-
     fare since 1945*. New York: Harmony Books, 1981.
Timmerman, Frederick W., Jr., Col. "Future Warriors." *Military Review*
     67 (September 1987): 46–55.
Toffler, Alvin and Heidi. *War and Anti-War: Survival at the Dawn of the
     21st Century*. New York: Little Brown, 1993.
Toguchim, Robert M., Maj., and James Hogue. "The Battle of Conver-
     gence in Four Dimensions." *Military Review* 72 (October 1992):
     11–20.
Townshend, Charles. *Britain's Civil Wars: Counterinsurgency in the Twen-
     tieth Century*. London: Faber & Faber, 1986.
Uhlig, Frank, Jr. *How Navies Fight: The U.S. Navy and Its Allies*. Annapolis,
     Md.: Naval Institute Press, 1994.
U.S. Military Academy, Department of History. *History of Revolutionary
     Warfare*. 6 vols., text material, USMA, 1967–77.
War in Peace: Conventional and Guerrilla Warfare since 1945. New York:
     Harmony, 1982.
Wilkins, Fred J., Lt. "The Guerrilla." *The Cavalry Journal* 50 (September–
     October 1941): 22–25.
Young, Marilyn B. *The Vietnam Wars 1945–1990*. New York: HarperCol-
     lins, 1991.

Index